ALWYN
CRAWSHAW
PAINTS
OILS

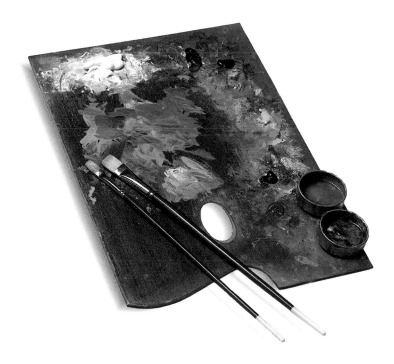

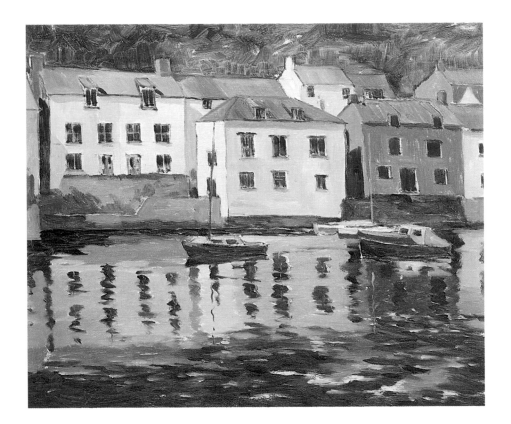

ALWYN CRAWSHAW

PAINTS

OILS

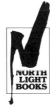

North Light Books
Cincinnati, Ohio

First published in U.S.A. in 1993 by
North Light Books, an imprint of
F&W Publications, 1507 Dana Avenue,
Cincinnati, OH 45207 (1-800-289-0963)

First published in the UK in 1992 by
HarperCollins Publishers
London

© Alwyn Crawshaw, 1992

Consultant Editor: Flicka Lister

Designed and typeset by Terry Jeavons

Photography: Nigel Cheffers-Heard
Location photographs: David John Hare and
June Crawshaw

**A catalogue record for this book is available
from the British Library.**

Jacket photograph of the author by Nigel
Cheffers-Heard.

ISBN 0-89134-537-X

Printed and bound in the UK

ACKNOWLEDGEMENTS

Firstly I would like to offer my grateful thanks to
David Hare, the producer, Ingrid Duffell, the
director, and all the television crew of *Crawshaw
Paints Oils* for their professionalism and
understanding during the making of the
television series.

I am indebted to Cathy Gosling from
HarperCollins, to Flicka Lister for the editing
of this book, and also to Gertrude Young and
Mary Poole for typing the manuscript. Finally
I would like to thank June, my wife, for all her
help and support.

The eight-part television series, *Crawshaw Paints
Oils*, was produced by David John Hare for
TSW – Television South West.

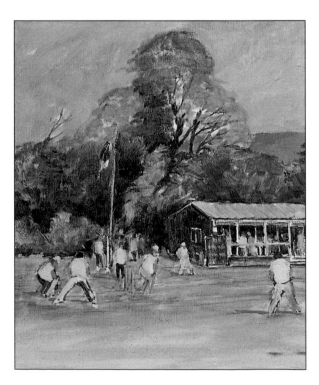

CONTENTS

PORTRAIT OF
THE ARTIST

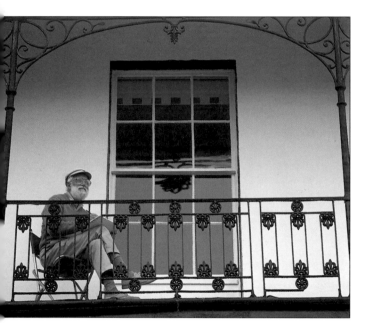

Successful painter, author and teacher Alwyn Crawshaw was born at Mirfield, Yorkshire, and studied at Hastings School of Art. He now lives in Dawlish, Devon, with his wife June, where they have opened their own gallery. As well as painting in oils, Alwyn also works in watercolour, acrylics and pastels. He is a Fellow of the Royal Society of Arts and a member of the Society of Equestrian Artists and the British Watercolour Society.

Alwyn's previous books for HarperCollins include eight in their *Learn to Paint* series, *The Artist at Work* (an autobiography of his painting career), *Sketching with Alwyn Crawshaw*, *The Half-Hour Painter*, *Alwyn Crawshaw's Watercolour Painting Course* and *Alwyn Crawshaw's Oil Painting Course*.

Alwyn's best selling book *A Brush with Art* accompanied his first 12-part Channel Four television series in 1991, a second book, *Crawshaw Paints on Holiday*, accompanied his second 6-part Channel Four series, and this book, *Crawshaw Paints Oils*, is the third Channel Four television series with a tie-in book of the same title.

Alwyn has been a guest on local and national radio programmes, including *The Gay Byrne Radio Show* in Eire, and has appeared on various television programmes, including BBC Television's *Pebble Mill at One*, *Daytime Live* and *Spotlight South West*. Alwyn has made several successful videos on painting and in 1991 was listed as one of the top ten artist video teachers in America. He is also a regular contributor to *Leisure Painter* magazine. Alwyn organises his own painting courses and holidays as well as giving demonstrations and lectures to art groups and societies throughout Britain.

Fine art prints of Alwyn's well-known

paintings are in demand worldwide. His paintings are sold in British and overseas galleries and can be found in private collections throughout the world. Alwyn has exhibited at the Royal Society of British Artists in London, and he won the prize for the best watercolour on show at the Society of Equestrian Artists' 1986 Annual Exhibition. He is listed in the current edition of *Who's Who in Art*.

Heavy working horses and elm trees are frequently featured in Alwyn's paintings and may be considered the artist's trademark. Painted mainly from nature and still life, Alwyn's work has been favourably reviewed by critics. *The Telegraph Weekend Magazine* reported him to be 'a landscape painter of considerable expertise' and *The Artist's and Illustrator's Magazine* described him as 'outspoken about the importance of maintaining traditional values in the teaching of art'.

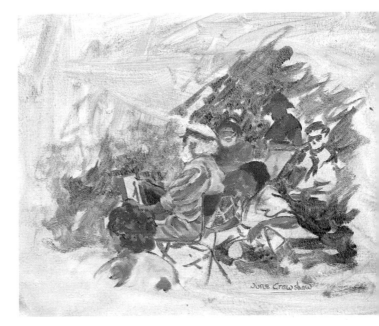

Sketch of Alwyn with students by June Crawshaw

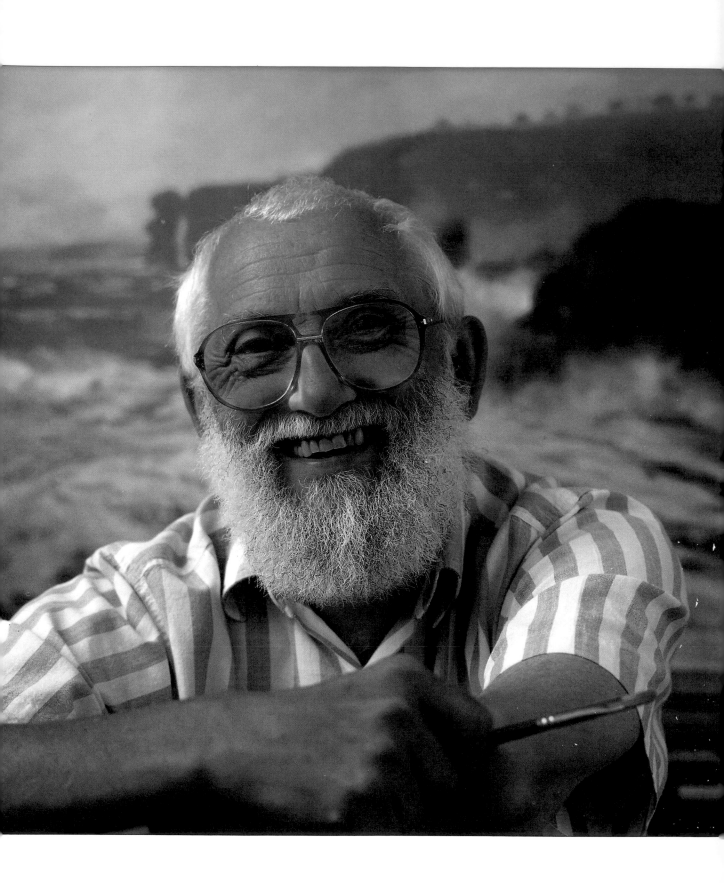

INTRODUCTION

'I can't paint – I'm not an artist.' People have said this to me many, many times. When I ask, 'Have you tried, the answer is usually no! However, when I ask the question, 'Can you drive a car?', a non-driver will usually reply, 'No, but I haven't had any lessons.' Well, the same applies to painting! If you haven't had any painting lessons, how can you know if you could be an artist or not?

Of course – before you try – you need to be inspired enough to have a go, and that is the object of this book and of my television series, Crawshaw Paints Oils. My aim is both to inspire you and to teach you the basic principles of oil painting. I also hope to encourage you to practise by yourself and improve your painting skills. This is so important. The more you practise, the more confidence you will gain and the more you will enjoy your painting.

So, if you have ever had a secret desire to try oil painting but always lacked confidence, why not look over my shoulder and share my thoughts as I paint? Then pick up a brush yourself and don't be shy – simply have a go. It's easier than you think and it will reward you with hours of enjoyment. But don't forget to practise!

Alwyn Crawshaw

MATERIALS

Those of you who haven't painted in oils before are probably a little confused about what you need to buy, just to get started. You may not know how to mix the paint, what to mix it on – or what to mix it with! For this reason, the following gives you a brief summary of the oil painting sequence.

You buy your oil paint in tubes, squeeze it on to a palette, then mix the paints with a brush. As you mix you add a medium to your paints with your brush – either one to thin the paint or another to make the paint spread more easily. (I use a medium in this way that also helps the paint to dry more quickly.) Then you brush the paint onto your working surface and you're painting! It really is as simple as that for you to get started. Naturally, as you progress, there are hundreds of variations to this sequence, but leave all that to time and experience!

The most frightening part of painting for students and beginners is that blank canvas or board staring at you before you start work. Even professionals can feel intimidated by it. When I have a large canvas to start in the studio and I am hesitating, my wife June says, 'You're doing a war dance round it, aren't you!' War dance or not, there's only one way to get over it – put some paint on and get started! The consolation with oil paint is that you can always wipe paint off and start again if you don't like your first brush strokes.

COLOURS

There are two qualities of oil paints: Artists' Professional quality and students' colours. The former are more expensive. I used Georgian Oil Colours, a students' quality, for all the paintings in the series and I am sure you will find them perfectly adequate. Illustrated on the palette opposite are the colours I use for my oil painting. Clockwise, from the top left, they are: Titanium White, Gel medium for drying the paint, Cobalt Blue, Viridian (green), Yellow Ochre, Cadmium Yellow, Crimson Alizarin and Cadmium Red.

All artists use their own range of colours, and no doubt you will want to try other colours. Start by using those I have recommended – your experience will take you on to other colours.

It is important to put each colour in the same position on the palette each time. You must be able to put the brush into the colour you want without having to think about it so that it becomes second nature. I don't use black paint, in whatever medium I am working. I believe that if it is on your palette you tend to use it to darken colours and this can make them 'dirty' or lifeless. I mix my 'blacks' (dark colours) by using the three primary colours – red, yellow, blue – and this keeps the 'black' lively not dull. If you want to use black I suggest you first gain experience in mixing colours from the three primaries; this is explained on page 23.

My oil painting palette ▶

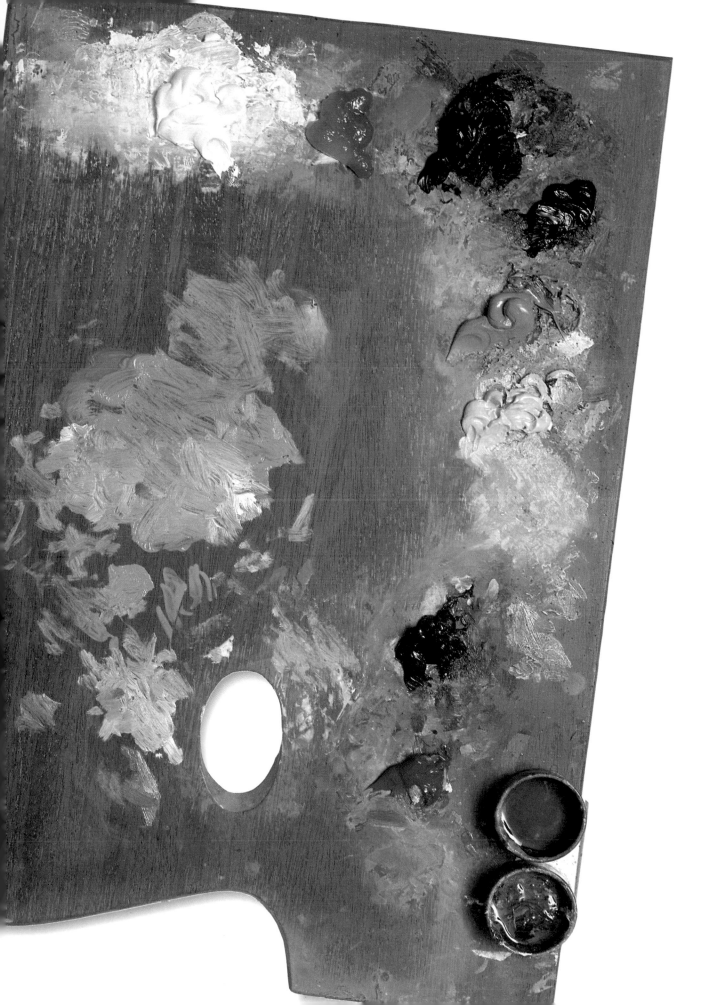

BRUSHES

It is the brush that makes the marks on the canvas, joining them together to create the picture, so the choice of brush is important. However, a brush that suits one artist does not suit another. If you are a beginner, I suggest you use the brushes that I used throughout the television series until you have gained more experience, see Basic kit, page 15.

For oil painting there are three basic brush shapes: round, filbert and flat (sometimes referred to as 'square'). These are shown below. I prefer the flat brush for general work. The traditional oil painting brush is usually made from hog bristles, but today man-made (nylon) bristles are used – not necessarily to replace the hog bristles but to allow the artist more scope. For detail work I use a small round sable brush and a nylon rigger, also shown. Series of brushes for oil colours start at No. 1 (the smallest) and usually continue up to No. 12 (the largest). You must keep your brushes clean by washing them first in turpentine substitute (white spirit) and then with soap, after a painting session. Put some soap in the palm of your hand and rub the brush into it under cold running water. Thoroughly rinse and dry the brushes before you use them again. While you are working, of course, you should only clean your brushes with turpentine substitute.

PALETTE KNIFE

A palette knife is used for mixing large quantities of paint on the palette (I prefer to mix with my brush, and did so for all the work in the television series), for cleaning paint off the palette, and for scraping paint off the canvas if the paint is too thick or if you want to repaint a certain part of the work.

The palette knife is a general purpose tool, and you will doubtless find other uses for it when you are painting.

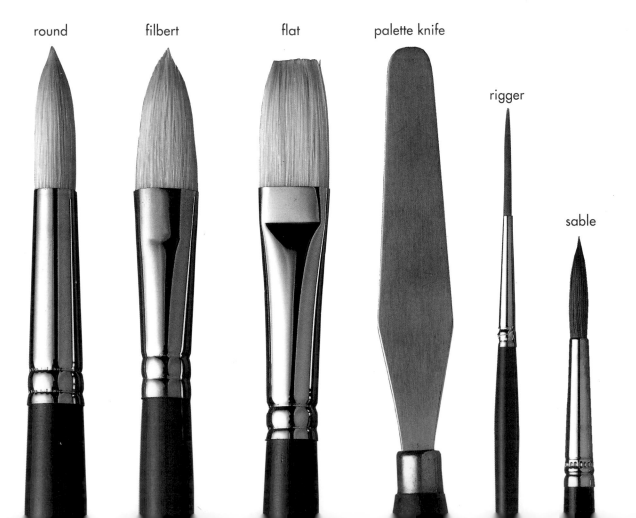

round   filbert   flat   palette knife   rigger   sable

PAINTING SURFACES

The traditional painting surface (support) for oil painting is canvas but, over the years, new surfaces have emerged which are cheaper and allow the artist more choice.

When you buy a canvas it has usually been primed and stretched ready to use. This is the most expensive surface to work on. I suggest that to start with you work on other supports and use canvas only for a few 'special' paintings.

On this page some painting surfaces are reproduced actual size. I have also applied some paint to help show you the grain of each surface. All absorbent surfaces, such as paper or hardboard, must be primed so that the oil from the paint is not sucked into it, see page 34.

Canvas boards are simply boards with canvas, already primed and stuck on to one side. A canvas panel has a simulated canvas surface. Oil sketching paper(rough and smooth grain) is one of the most inexpensive supports; I used a great deal of it at art school. It is primed and ready to work on, and can be bought in pads or sheets. I discuss other working surfaces on page 34.

When I organized and judged a painting competition for my local BBC radio station, one artist sent in a painting done on the back of one side of a cornflakes box. Obviously it had been primed and it gave a reasonable support. I don't know what would be the life of such a painting, but it shows what you could use to practise some basic brush strokes and colour mixing, although I wouldn't recommend it for serious paintings. Try different supports to find the one you prefer.

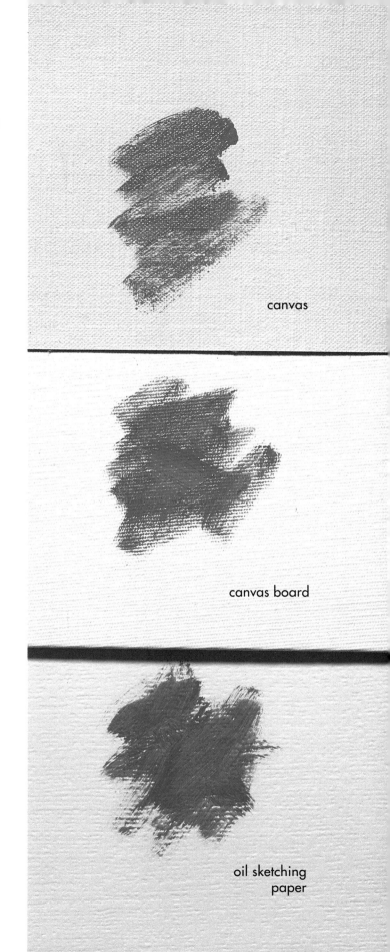

canvas

canvas board

oil sketching
paper

MEDIUMS

There are many different mediums on the market which you mix with the paint either to thin it down or to make it spread more easily. You put your medium in a receptacle called a 'dipper'. You can get them as a single dipper or a double dipper, shown on the opposite page. They slide onto your palette and are held firmly in place while you paint.

Turpentine is used to thin down the paint, in particular for underpainting or painting thin lines. Don't confuse this with turpentine substitute (white spirit) which you can buy from your local hardware store and which you use to clean your brushes and palette. If you find the smell of turpentine too strong, you can use Low Odour Oil Painting Thinners instead, as I do; this doesn't smell. Because oil paint takes a long time to dry, I use Alkyd Medium, a jelly-like liquid which halves the drying time of oil paint and also helps spread the paint. Another drying agent, Gel Medium, is available in a tube. I squeeze this onto my palette for working, see page 11.

To sum up, I use only Low Odour Oil Painting Thinners (instead of turpentine) and Alkyd or Gel Medium for all my paintings. I suggest you use these two or three only; they make oil painting simpler.

EASELS

A good strong easel is important because your painting surface must be firm and rigid. If you haven't the room for a standing easel, then a table one is sufficient. You can even put your support on the seat of a kitchen chair and rest it against the back. On page 77 you can see the easel I used for Programme 8, when painting the cricket match at Ottery St Mary.

Easels vary so much in size, type and cost that I can only suggest you try some out for yourself in an art supply shop. Choose one that is steady and, when folded up for use outdoors, is comfortable to carry.

CARRYING BOX

For all the outdoor work in the television series, except for Programme 8, I used a pochade box and not an easel. This takes boards up to 25 × 30 cm (10 × 12 in). The painting board slots into the lid and you rest the box on your knees to paint. You can see me working with it below and in some of the photos at the back of the book. The lid slides off the box with a palette attached to it, and the main box area carries all the equipment and paints you need. It packs away into a neat case that you can carry by hand, just like a small briefcase.

After making the series, I decided to design a smaller one, the Oil Travelling Studio, which is now on the market. This can be carried over your shoulder, making it even more portable for holidays and impromptu days out sketching. It takes two boards 15 × 20 cm (6 × 8 in) for painting on and contains all the materials you need. The shoulder strap can also be worn around the neck to support the kit, so you can even paint standing up with it.

▼ Working with my pochade box

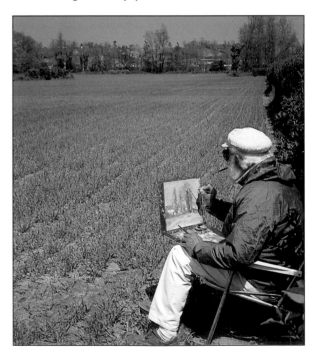

PALETTES

Palettes are either oval or oblong and are made from wood or white plastic. The oval ones are called studio palettes but oblong ones are the most popular. Some artists use glass placed on top of a table. You must keep the mixing area clean with turpentine substitute after each painting session. Naturally, if you use a pochade box or the Oil Travelling Studio, you don't need a separate palette for it.

BASIC KIT

Shown below are the basic materials you need to start oil painting.
The Georgian Oil Colours that I use are listed on page 10. The brushes you need are: Rowney Bristlewhite Series B.48 Nos. 1, 2, 4 and 6, a sable brush Series 43 No. 6 and a Dalon Rigger Series D.99 No. 2. When you have become familiar with these you can experiment with different ones. If you wish you can buy two

brushes of each size, one for dark and the other for light colours. This saves having to wash the brush free of paint already mixed but, if you're like me, you'll start that way and then find you've put the 'dark' brush into the light colour and vice versa!

You will also need a palette, a palette knife with a 7.5 cm (3 in) blade; turpentine or Low Odour Oil Painting Thinners, a bottle of Alkyd Medium and a double dipper for your palette to hold each of them – alternatively use a tube of Gel Medium; a mahl stick for steadying your brush, see page 30; an old jam jar for turpentine substitute to wash out your brushes; canvas boards or your chosen support; a paint rag for wiping and cleaning your brushes and hands; and finally a plastic eraser and an HB pencil.

To save money you can buy the minimum number of brushes, find your own receptacles to hold the mediums and use a piece of formica or varnished plywood as a palette and a kitchen chair as an easel. *Don't be afraid to improvise!*

▼ The basic materials you need to start oil painting.

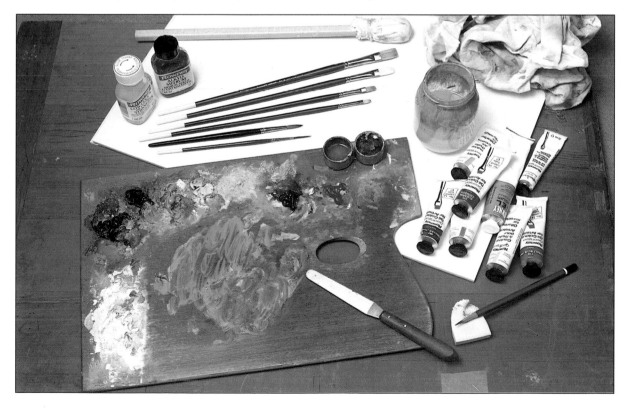

THE 8 PROGRAMMES

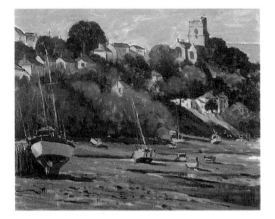

NEWTON FERRERS
OBSERVATION

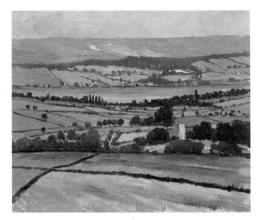

WOODBURY COMMON
COLOUR MIXING

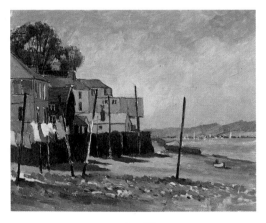

LYMPSTONE
BRUSH STROKES

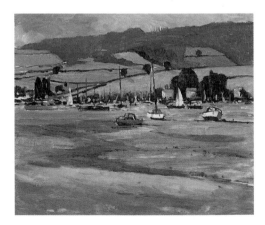

EXMOUTH
WORKING SURFACES

A course of easy-to-follow oil painting lessons
to accompany the television series

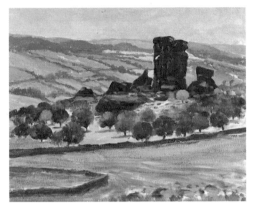

VIXEN TOR
DRAWING IN YOUR SUBJECT

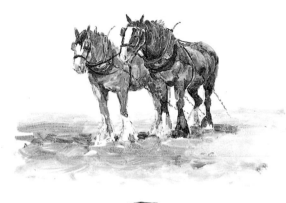

SHIRE HORSE CENTRE
PAINTING HORSES

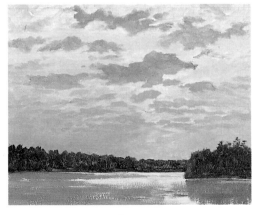

STUDIO
WORKING FROM PHOTOGRAPHS

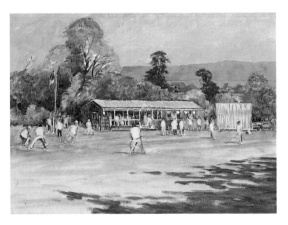

OTTERY ST MARY
PAINTING PEOPLE AND TREES

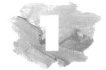

NEWTON FERRERS

OBSERVATION

One of the myths attached to oil painting is the belief that you must paint on huge canvases in a large studio, using a lot of paint and surrounded by mountains of equipment. If you visit a major public art gallery, most of the oil paintings on display are large – some big enough to cover a whole wall in an average house! The image that this creates is enough to make you believe that all oil paintings must be large in scale. However, remember that most of these are by the Old Masters and professional artists, not leisure painters. *You* can paint with a fraction of their space and equipment, and you don't have to paint on big canvases.

Some of our most famous artists have worked very small in oil paint. For example, John Constable, one of Britain's best-known landscape artists went outdoors painting and sketching with sizes ranging from about 15 × 10 cm (6 × 4 in). In fact, some people prefer those small sketches to his full-size studio paintings. Sadly, in public galleries, it is usually the larger, more impressive works that are on the walls, unless a special exhibition is being held.

Of course, if you want to paint big and you have the space, don't let me stop you. However, for this television series – except for the painting in the last programme, which was 40 × 60 cm (16 × 24 in) – I worked all my paintings 25 × 30 cm (10 × 12in). I did this to let you see how exciting it can be to work small. Depending on your ability and the subject, you should be able to finish a painting this size in an hour and a

half to three hours. But, above all, when working at this size, a beginner won't get impatient or bored.

So you don't need to paint big and your equipment can be reasonably simple and easy to carry (see the pochade box that I use, on page 14). You don't need to use a lot of paint, either – I don't. In fact, I'm what I consider to be a thin oil painter. I apply thin paint to start with, and use thicker paint for lighter colours and highlights as my painting progresses.

In the chapters that follow, I go into detail about colour mixing, brushes to use, surfaces to work on, and many other aspects of oil painting. I have also highlighted some of the most important and interesting aspects of the paintings that I did for the television series, with close-up details to help you see exactly how these were achieved. *The size of all the close-up details has been enlarged by 20 per cent.* Reproducing them slightly larger than their real-life size will enable you to see the brush strokes and thickness or thinness of the paint more clearly. I hope that this will help you to see more precisely how I painted each picture.

One of the most important aspects of painting is the ability to 'see'. It isn't enough to glance at your subject casually – you need to really observe and understand it to paint it well. Observation is fundamental to painting, whatever medium you are working in. As a casual onlooker, from your deck chair on the beach, you might see two children running down to the water. As an artist, you would see that one of the children was a girl with blonde hair wearing a red costume and waterproof

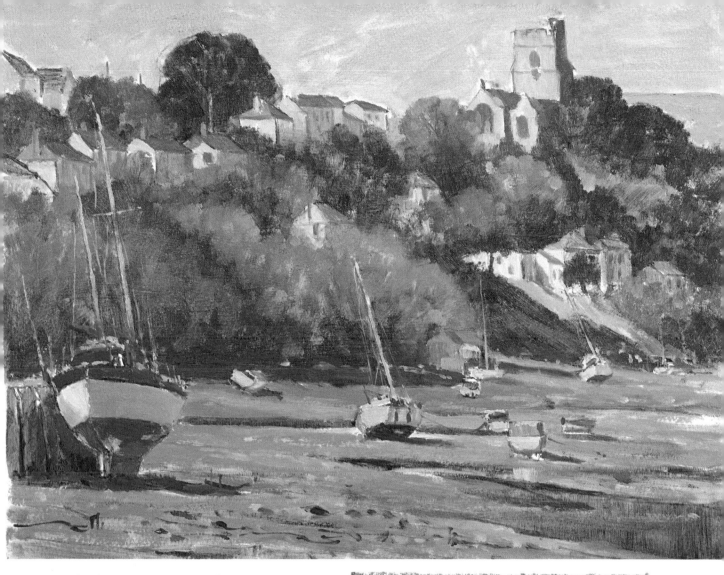

Primed Whatman paper 200 lb Not,
25 × 30 cm (10 × 12 in)

shoes. You would also observe that her
companion was a boy wearing a blue costume
and carrying a bucket in each hand, while the
girl was carrying two spades, both in her right
hand. You would have noticed the way their
footprints looked in the wet sand, and also have
seen their reflections, the colour of the sea and
the dry sand, and so on. In other words, to be an
artist, you have to observe the scene properly in
order to be able to put it down on paper. Start
practising, even now, as you read this book.
Look about you and observe. You will be
surprised how soon you will learn to see with an
artist's eye. When I did the painting for this first
programme at Newton Ferrers, there was plenty
for me to observe!

PAINTING TIPS

The tide comes up quickly in an estuary
and changes the scene. You must be able
to work very quickly, or paint a small
size picture.

When painting a group of middle
distance trees in leaf, vary the greens that
you mix. This gives them 'life'.

Naturally always try, but don't worry if
you can't get the *exact* colour you are
copying from. It won't spoil your painting.

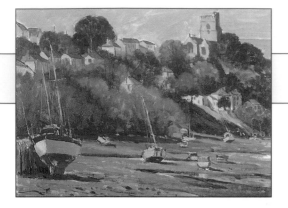

► The first thing to do was to observe the position of the sun. The sunlight was coming from the left, therefore the shadow was on the right side of the church and houses.

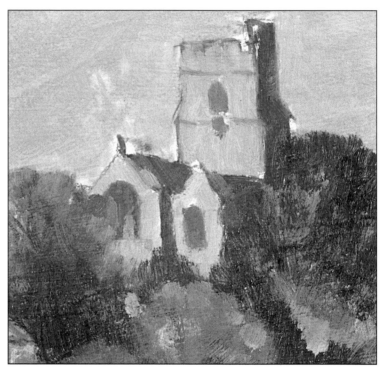

► Although I could see more detail in the houses in real life, I didn't paint it in. If I had, the houses would have been too prominent in the picture.

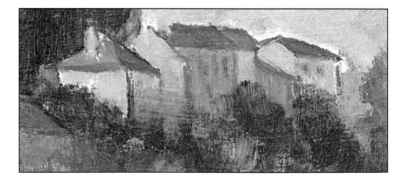

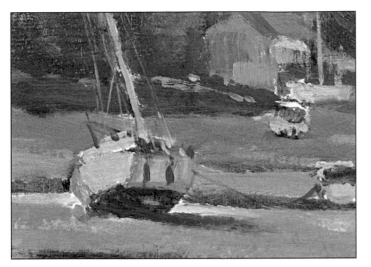

▲ Notice how the shadow is cast to the right of the yacht. This helps to sit the yacht firmly in the mud.

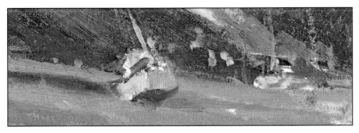

▲ As with the houses, I didn't put detail in this yacht.

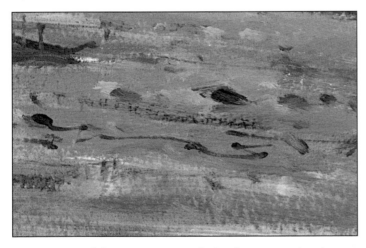

▲ I was careful not to overwork the foreground – this is important. Keep things simple and don't fiddle!

▶ Although this is a white yacht, look at how dark the shadow side is painted. This is the colour I *observed*, even though I knew the yacht was white.

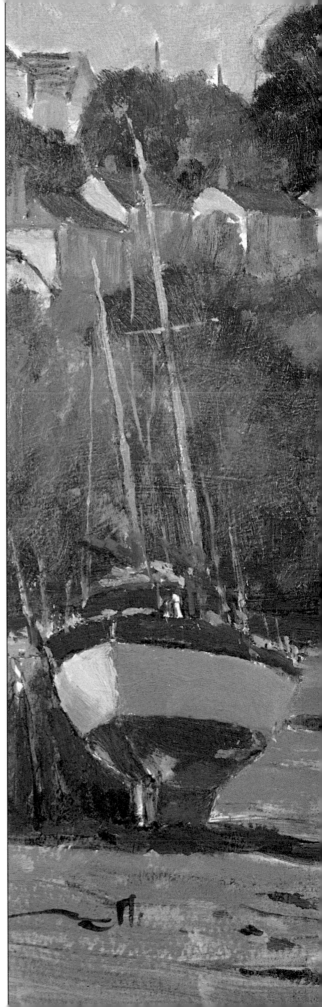

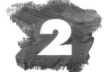

WOODBURY COMMON

COLOUR MIXING

Colour mixing is very important. There are thousands of colours around us if we really look, and this can be rather frightening for a beginner. Don't worry – nature has made it relatively easy for us! There are only three main colours and they cannot be mixed from any other colours. These are the primary colours: red, yellow and blue. By using a combination of these colours you can mix any colour that you see. There are many different colour reds, yellows and blues to help us, but I use only six colours plus Titanium White for most of my painting (see page 10). The colours I use most frequently are the three primaries, Crimson Alizarin, Cadmium Yellow and Cobalt Blue, shown at the top of the opposite page. I also use Cadmium Red, Yellow Ochre and a green called Viridian. The latter is my only 'ready-mixed' colour and I find it helps me to mix the different colour greens which are needed in landscape painting.

To make colours lighter with oil, you have to add white paint and to make colours darker you use less white paint or none at all. To mix the darkest colour, 'black', you mix the three primaries together, starting with blue, then adding a little red, and finally a little yellow (see the colour mixing chart opposite).

The secret of successful colour mixing is to always start with the predominant colour of the mix. For instance, if you want a yellowy-green, the predominant colour will be yellow. Blue and yellow make green, therefore you put yellow (the predominant colour) onto your palette, and add a *little* blue. This makes a yellowy-green. If you put the blue in first, you will have to add a lot more yellow to make a yellowy-green, waste a lot of paint and time, and perhaps have lost your patience before you achieve the colour you want. So it is *very* important that the predominant colour is put on your palette first and you mix a smaller amount of the second or third primary colour into it, until you obtain your required colour.

Practise at home mixing colours. You don't need to paint big areas – go for the size of the colours opposite. Make notes of which colours you mix and roughly the amounts of each colour – it will help you to remember what you have done. Although mixing colours can be frustrating at first, everyone can learn and, in time, it will become second nature to you. But you must practise!

HOW TO MIX PRIMARY COLOURS

THE THREE PRIMARY COLOURS

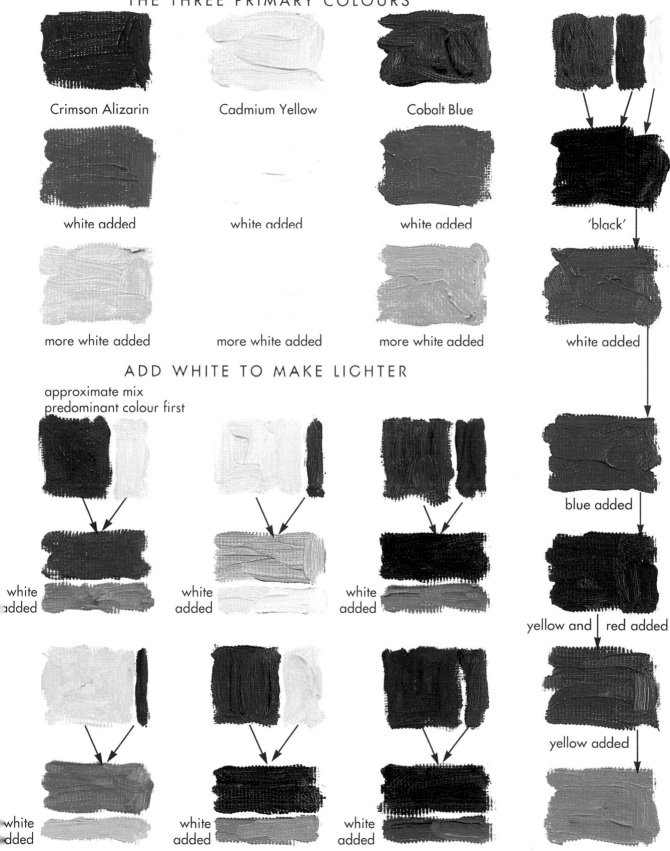

Crimson Alizarin

Cadmium Yellow

Cobalt Blue

white added

white added

white added

'black'

more white added

more white added

more white added

white added

ADD WHITE TO MAKE LIGHTER

approximate mix
predominant colour first

white
added

white
added

white
added

blue added

white
added

white
added

white
added

yellow and | red added

yellow added

white added

HOW TO MIX GREENS FOR LANDSCAPE

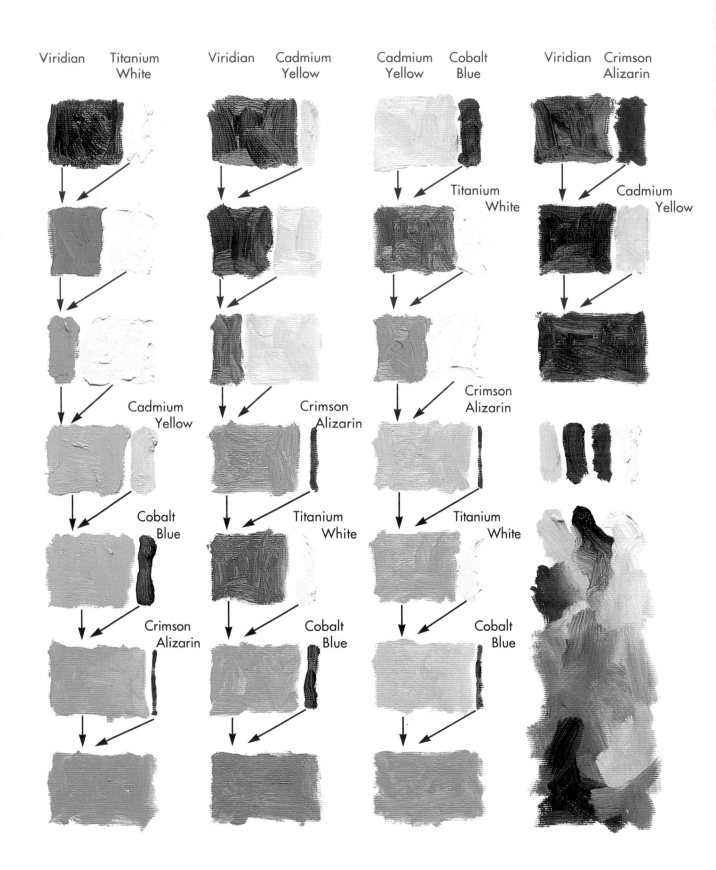

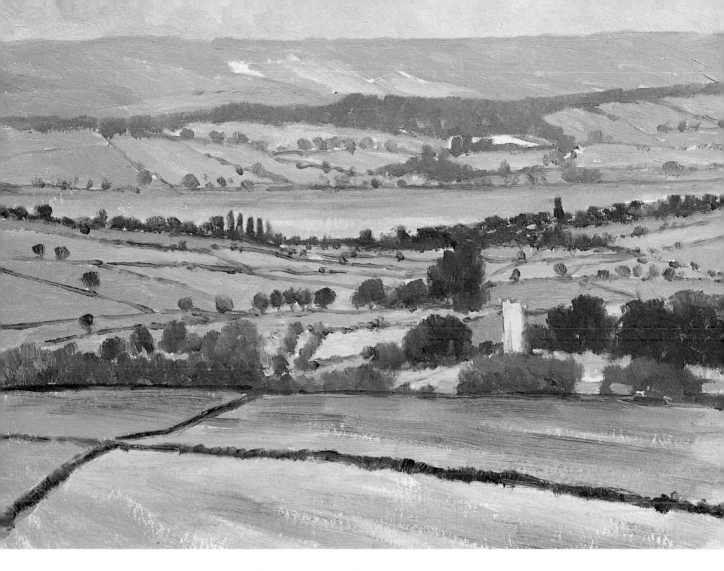

Primed Whatman paper 200 lb Not with a Yellow Ochre wash, 25 x 30 cm (10 x 12 in)

The view from Woodbury Common can be breathtaking but I chose this scene because, although there is a lot 'happening' in it, the detail work is very simple. In a scene like this, if a field is positioned too low or too high on your canvas, no one will notice, and it won't spoil your picture. Many of the trees are single brush strokes, and even the church has no features painted onto it. So with this scene, I concentrated on the picture as a whole, and on the different greens.

Students usually find mixing different colour greens for landscape painting quite difficult. The problem is that, if the greens are not subtly different from one another, the landscape can look flat, lifeless and uninteresting. Some professionals also find it difficult, and I'm no exception. As I have said, with oils I use a ready-mixed green to help me – I also use one with my watercolour and acrylic painting.

On the chart opposite you can see how I've used it with white and my primary colours to mix some different greens. Remember, the amounts used are just as important whether the desired effect is subtle or dramatic.

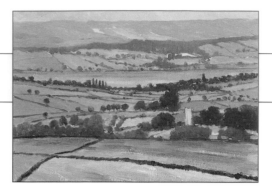

► In reality, distant green colours tend to lose their brightness and appear 'cooler'. To portray this, you need to add blue.

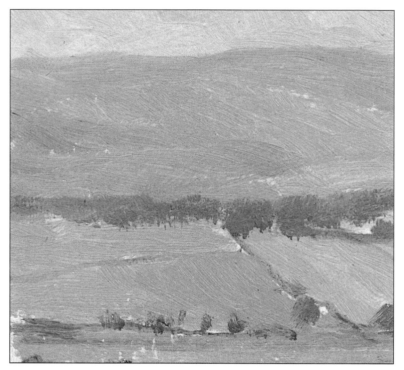

► These trees were created by single brush strokes of dark colour, mixed from the three primary colours.

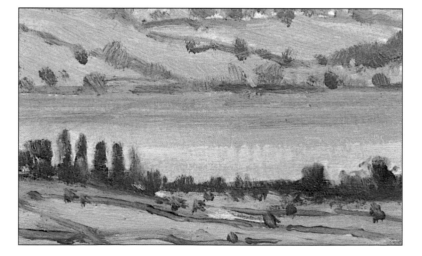

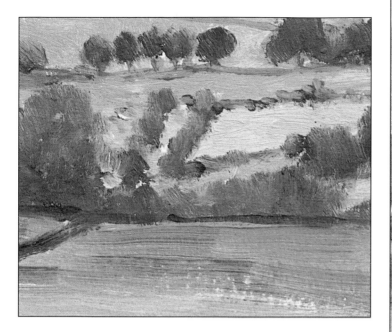

▲ Scale is always very important. The suggestion of trunks on these trees has helped to give scale to this part of the painting.

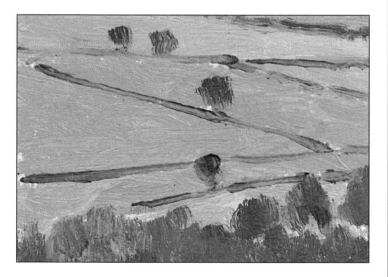

▲ Don't try to copy the shape of fields *exactly*. There is no real value in doing this.

▶ I started by positioning the church and then the estuary. Notice how there is no detail on the church tower. I painted dark fields and trees behind the church to give contrast – light (church) against dark (fields).

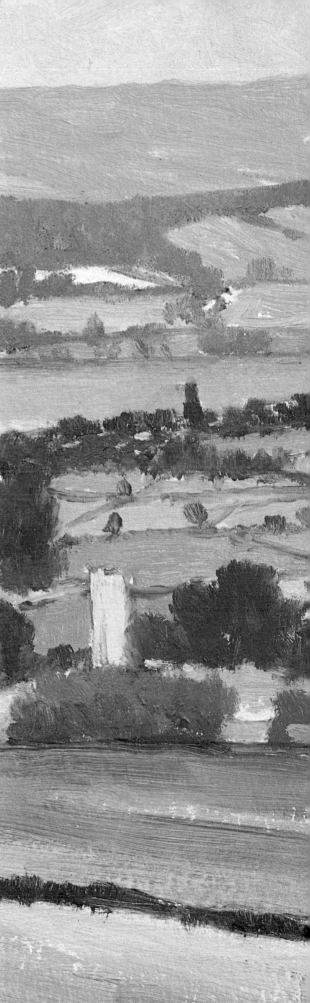

LYMPSTONE

BRUSH STROKES

Because the brush plays such an important role in a painting, the more you practise with it the more you will learn what it can do and the better your painting will be. This in turn will give you the confidence to relax and really enjoy painting. So you can't practise enough!

On the opposite page, I show three basic ways of holding your brush and the brush strokes they will give you. If you get used to these, other ways will develop naturally as you practise and gain experience.

For the 'flat hold', the brush is placed across the palm of the hand and held firmly by the thumb and first finger. This makes it easy to work over large areas, and allows you a lot of freedom with the brush strokes. But you don't have much control. Use this for underpainting, backgrounds, skies – areas where you want freedom and not detail.

For controlled painting areas, use the 'long hold'. Hold your brush as you would a pen or pencil, but not close to the bristles. Hold it 10-13 cm (4-5 in) away from them. Holding the brush this way allows you control over the strokes but enough movement of the brush to have freedom and movement over the canvas. You will find that you hold your brush in this way for most of a painting.

Finally I show the way to hold the brush for maximum control and detail work – the 'short hold'. Hold it just as you would a pen or pencil, but this time hold it close to the bristles for the greatest control. When you paint detail work with a sable or nylon brush, thin the paint with turpentine or medium to make it more 'runny', to allow it to flow out of the bristles.

Why don't you practise these brush strokes without paint first, and get used to working with the brush? Your brush strokes will either be delicate, vigorous, hesitant, heavy, flowing or flamboyant – it all depends on you, the way you are made and think. This is what helps to make all artists' work different so, as your own personal brush strokes develop and become natural to you, do keep them that way – it will help to make your paintings individual.

First practise these three basic brush holds – then create your own. ▶

28

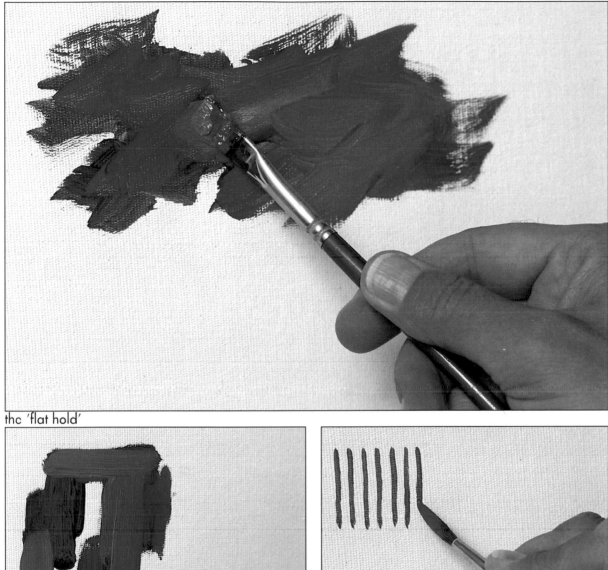

the 'flat hold'

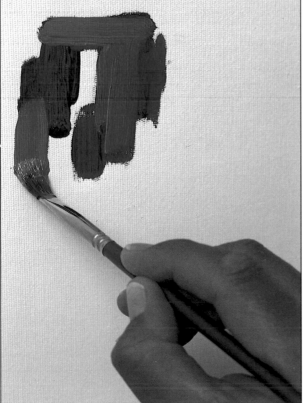

the 'long
hold'

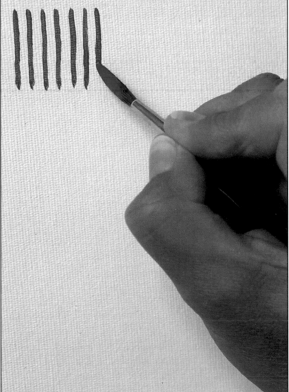

the 'short
hold'

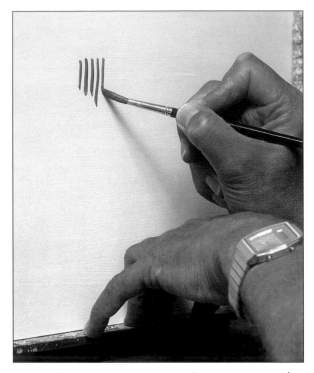

To avoid smudging wet paint when painting with a pochade box, use your other hand as a bridge.

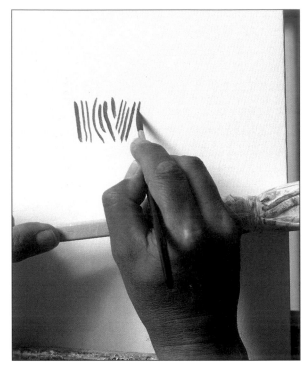

When working at an easel, use a mahl stick to rest your painting hand on.

During painting you will need to support your painting hand over wet areas of paint so that you don't smudge them. When you are using the pochade box, you can use your other hand as a bridge to rest your brush hand on, *above left*.

On larger work you will need a 'mahl stick' to rest your painting hand on. This is placed anywhere that is comfortable; on the painting (dry areas) or on the easel, *above right*. A mahl stick is usually made by fastening a piece of rag to one end of a long wooden stick. Mine is 38 cm (15 in) long.

When you work on very big canvases, you need a longer mahl stick.

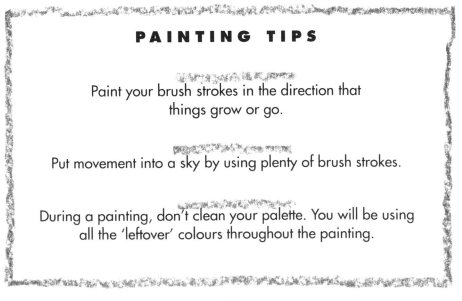

PAINTING TIPS

Paint your brush strokes in the direction that things grow or go.

Put movement into a sky by using plenty of brush strokes.

During a painting, don't clean your palette. You will be using all the 'leftover' colours throughout the painting.

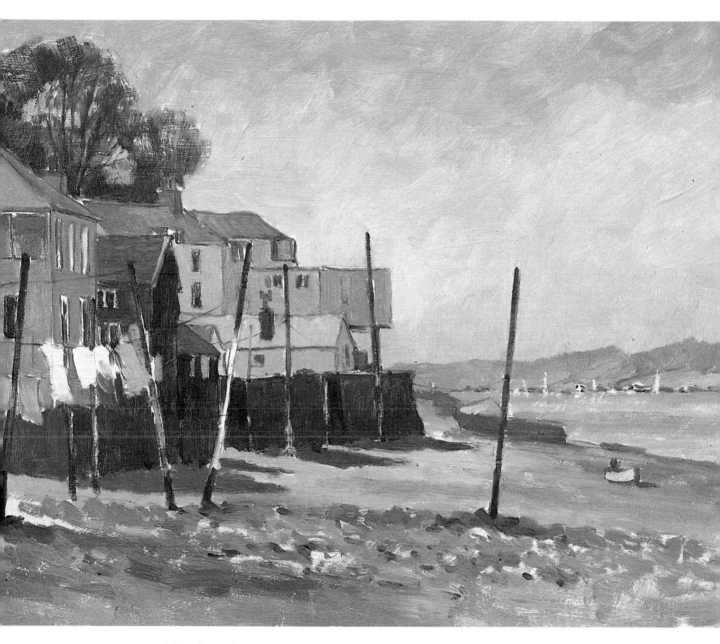

Primed hardboard with a Yellow Ochre wash, 25 × 30 cm (10 × 12 in)

Lympstone, on the river Exe estuary, made a very warm, colourful painting. One of the things that helped this was the contrast of the strong shadows cast by the dark sea wall against the brightly sunlit yellow beach area. The washing hanging on the line in front of the dark background also gave tremendous contrast, helping to create the illusion of sunlight. To the right of the washing, the pole with sunlight reflecting on it was achieved by leaving it unpainted throughout the painting. I simply painted around it.

Whatever you do, when you are painting buildings like this, don't become too involved with detail. Keep them simple. If you are not yet confident about your drawing ability, then I would suggest that you avoid painting subjects such as these until you have had more experience. But why not have a go and copy mine? It will help you in the meantime.

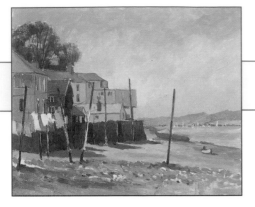

► I didn't paint any detail into the trees, except for some simple branches, using the 'short hold' brush stroke. I painted sky colour into the trees to show 'holes' in the foliage.

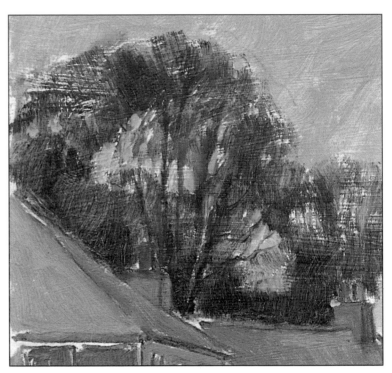

► The strong shadows help to create sunlight by giving contrast between dark and light areas. The shadow colours were mixed from Cobalt Blue, Crimson Alizarin, and little touches of Yellow Ochre and Titanium White.

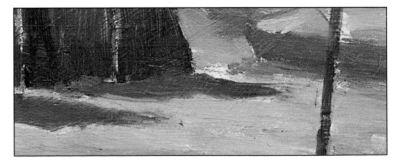

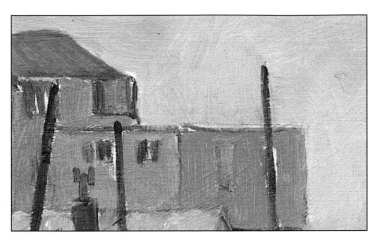

▲ Don't worry if your paint goes over edges or if it makes fuzzy lines.

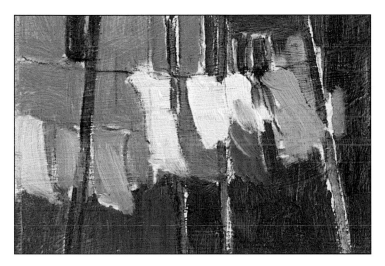

▲ The dark background contrasting against the bright washing on the line helps to bring the washing into the front of the picture, and also creates the illusion of sunshine.

▶ The sky was painted using the 'flat hold'. This gave movement to the brush strokes and life to the sky. The colours in the distant countryside were toned down and made cooler by adding blue. The suggestion of the yachts was done with single 'short hold' brush strokes. The side of the small white boat was painted in just one brush stroke – notice the direction it was done. The foreground beach area was kept very simple, using the 'long hold'.

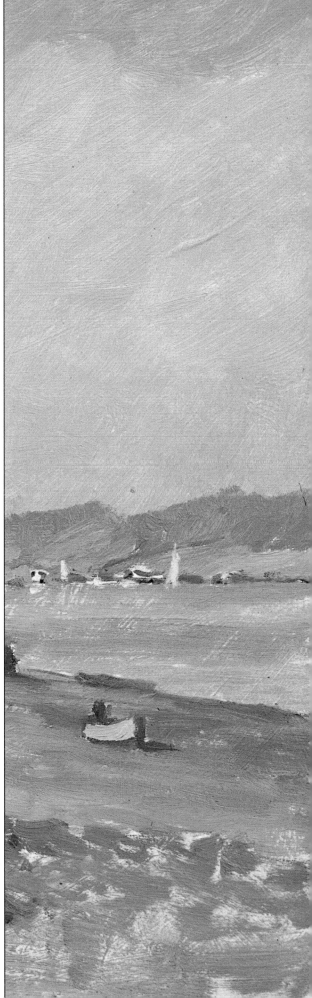

EXMOUTH

WORKING SURFACES

In the Materials section on page 13, I talked about canvas, canvas board and oil sketching paper. All those surfaces (supports) are already prepared to work on. But there are other less expensive surfaces that are very satisfactory for working on and, although you have to prepare them yourself, this is very easy.

The most common of these is hardboard. It must be interior quality, as exterior quality has been treated against outside conditions, and can harm the oil paint. It doesn't have to be a certain thickness or colour – some are light, others darker – and you prime it with three coats of Acrylic Primer or good quality emulsion paint. For large surfaces use a small household paintbrush and for small sizes use one of your larger oil painting brushes. You can make the surface very smooth or use your brush strokes to give it texture. I frequently use hardboard for small paintings up to 40 × 30 cm (16 × 12 in).

Another fairly inexpensive surface is watercolour paper. It must be primed in the same way as the hardboard, but it has the advantage of being lighter in weight for carrying. Usually I don't use it any larger than 25 × 30cm (10 × 12 in). It has a lovely surface to work on, depending on the paper you use. I use Whatman Watercolour paper 200 lb Not surface. Buy some different papers and try them out. You can even use cartridge drawing paper – about the least expensive of 'art' papers to buy. Again, this must

be primed with three coats of Acrylic Primer. Naturally, all papers must be rested against a board to give them stability when you work. Lightly stick the corners down and you shouldn't have any trouble.

Using paper isn't new. Some of John Constable's famous oil sketches were done on paper and these are still in good condition, over 200 years later. I often use paper for small outdoor work.

In addition to priming your surface with white Acrylic Primer, you can (when it's dry) paint over it with a 'wash' of oil colour paint mixed only with turpentine. I do this for two reasons. Firstly it takes the white glare off the blank surface when you start to paint – especially in strong sunlight – and secondly, where the colours don't completely cover the background, the underwash shows through and helps to unify the painting.

The colours most commonly used for this are a warm yellow or a blue-grey colour. I usually use Yellow Ochre, or mix it with a little Crimson Alizarin. It can help to give the painting a warm feeling. Remember that if you work your paint thinly it will show the underpainting through. You can also colour the surface with a wash of acrylic paint, which dries much quicker. Try a painting done on different colours – naturally you can use any colours you choose.

On the opposite page, different painting surfaces are reproduced and I have shown you what happens when you prime them, either by painting smoothly or to give a rough, textured effect. I have also put a colour wash on each of them to show you the difference it makes.

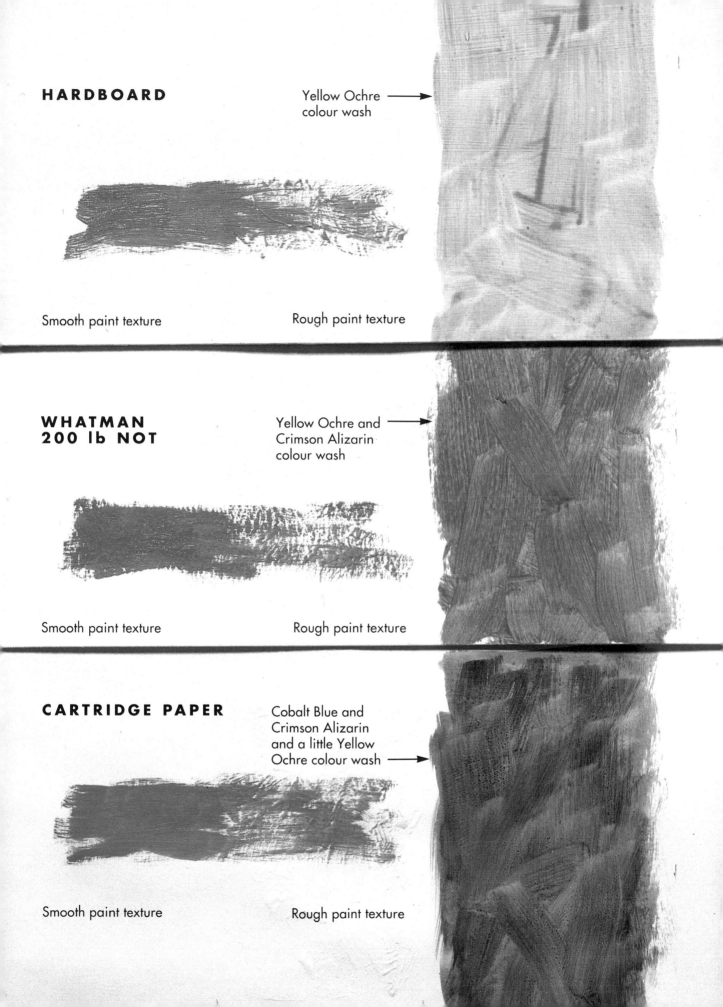

HARDBOARD

Yellow Ochre
colour wash →

Smooth paint texture

Rough paint texture

WHATMAN
200 lb NOT

Yellow Ochre and →
Crimson Alizarin
colour wash

Smooth paint texture

Rough paint texture

CARTRIDGE PAPER

Cobalt Blue and
Crimson Alizarin
and a little Yellow
Ochre colour wash →

Smooth paint texture

Rough paint texture

The biggest problem I had to overcome at Exmouth was what to paint. There was so much to tempt me from boats of all shapes and sizes that I could get close up to in the small harbour to the vast panorama across the estuary.

Presented with a choice of scenery like this, it's a good idea to sit down and relax for a moment and take a deep breath. Then look carefully at the scene again, this time searching for areas to paint. When painting an estuary scene, select a group of boats, a group of buildings or an interesting composition made by the mud banks, and use that as your painting.

I did just that with a section of the estuary at low water. I must admit I was disappointed that we didn't have a cloudy sky, as clouds give wonderful effects of dark shadows against sunlit areas. The estuary where I was working is very flat and the tide comes in extremely quickly, so I had to work fast. Even so, I wasn't quite quick enough to finish the painting before the tide came in around my feet. It's lucky that I have a good visual memory!

After drawing in with my brush, I started to paint the sky, then the forests and fields on the other side of the estuary. I then came to the distant shoreline and boats. When you look at an area like that, it is very complicated and difficult to define, no matter how clever you are at observation. You know the main objects are boats and trees, but when you look hard it still looks like 'nothing'. There's always a lot of 'nothingness' in most scenes – areas that you can't make out, where you can't understand what's going on. Well, simply paint what you see – paint an area of 'nothing'. You will be surprised – it will look fine on your painting, and look exactly like the scene in front of you.

I was a little concerned about the amount of mud area on the painting, as it could have looked a little uninteresting when I painted it. But by painting dark wet areas against the dry sunlit area in the foreground, I was very happy with the result.

If you look at the close-up details on pages 38 and 39, you will also see the texture of the surface that I made with my paintbrush when I primed the hardboard. This also helped to stop the mud from looking too flat and uninteresting.

I am always telling students, 'Keep objects simple, especially if they are not close to you'. Just look at all the boats in my painting and see how simply they are worked. This doesn't mean it's easy, but it's something you have to strive for in your painting, especially when you are working outdoors.

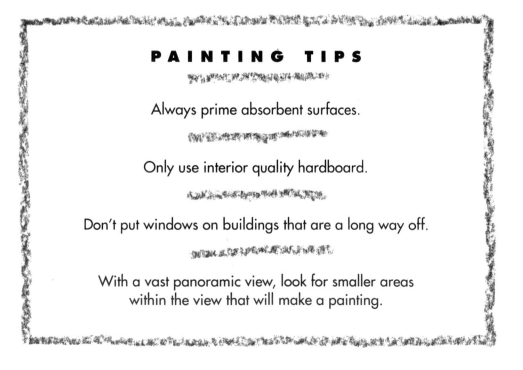

PAINTING TIPS

Always prime absorbent surfaces.

Only use interior quality hardboard.

Don't put windows on buildings that are a long way off.

With a vast panoramic view, look for smaller areas within the view that will make a painting.

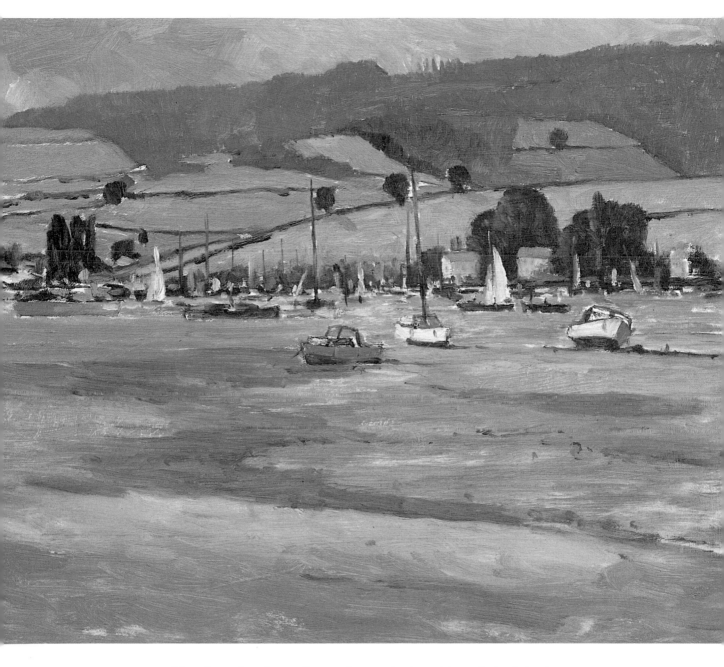

Primed hardboard with a Yellow Ochre wash, 25 × 30 cm (10 × 12 in)

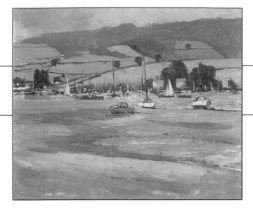

► This painting contains a good example of 'nothing-ness'. I knew it was made up of boats and trees, and so I used my brush to give the impression that boats and trees were there. The free brush stroke suggesting a yacht sail works well.

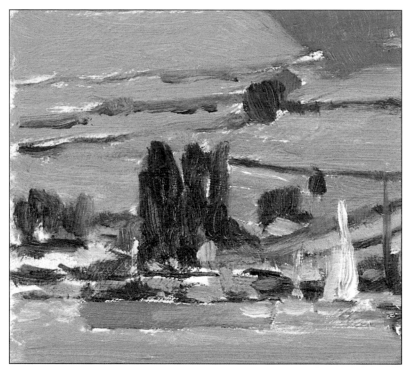

▼ Many of the brush strokes you can see on the board were done when I primed it. The contrast in the mud colours helps to make this area interesting and not 'flat'.

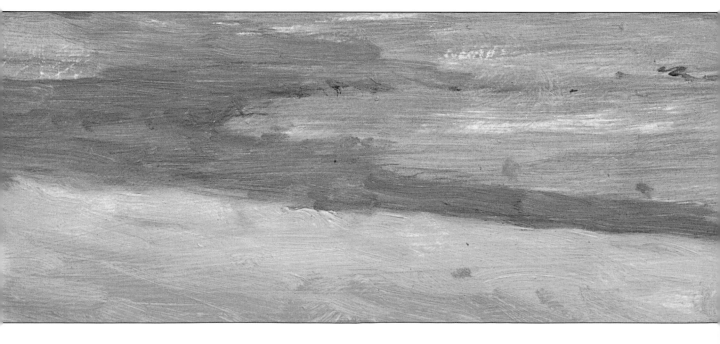

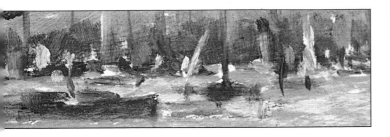

▲ Another example of 'nothingness' representing boats, water and trees, painted very freely.

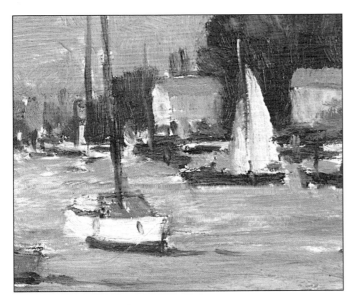

▲ This boat is closer than the background ones but it was still worked very freely. The side of it was painted with only one brush stroke.

▶ This helps to show how the darker, bluer colours of the hills and trees recede and the warmer colours of the beach and fields come forward. Notice how I didn't make the sails in the background as prominent as I did on the yacht in the first close-up.

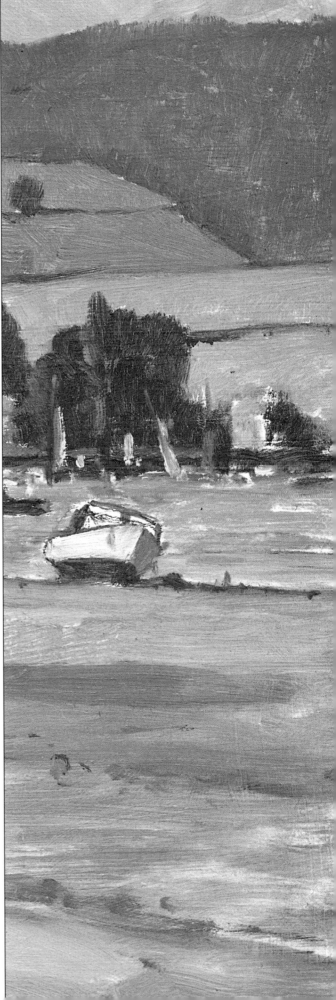

VIXEN TOR

DRAWING IN YOUR SUBJECT

There are four different ways of drawing in your painting before using paint in the normal way and these are shown on the opposite page. Although some artists don't bother to draw first, but start to paint straight onto the support, I don't suggest you do this unless you have had plenty of experience.

You can draw in the picture with a pencil, *above left*, but only go for main important lines. Don't draw any real detail

A common way of starting is to draw the picture with a brush, *above right*. I use Cobalt Blue and a little Crimson Alizarin mixed together with turpentine, so that it's like working with watercolour. It dries very quickly, in about 10 to 20 minutes. The blue line will show through in places and this helps to give your painting character. As you paint it also stays visible longer than a pencil line.

The third method, *below left*, is to paint in with a brush as before, then fill in the tonal values with the same colour, making them lighter by adding more turpentine, not by adding white paint. Don't paint the lightest areas – leave your support showing – but make sure you paint the 'very darks'.

Finally, you can draw in with a brush and then, with colours mixed with plenty of turpentine, paint in the picture, see *below right*. This mix is known as a 'turpsy wash'. Paint the picture as though you were painting it in

watercolour. Don't use white paint. Work very freely, don't give a thought to detail work and it will give you a perfect starting point. When you have done this you will be painting a scene that is by now familiar. This is very important as the more familiar you are with your subject the easier it is to paint. This naturally applies to professional painters as well as amateurs. You will also have a tonal guide and rough colour guide to work over.

If you discover your own way of starting a painting, then do use it. I am trying to put you on the road to oil painting, but if you find your own, congratulations! Keep going and enjoy it.

When we went to Dartmoor in Devon to film this programme, I explained these ways of starting a painting. The examples that I did for the television programme of Vixen Tor are shown on pages 42 and 43.

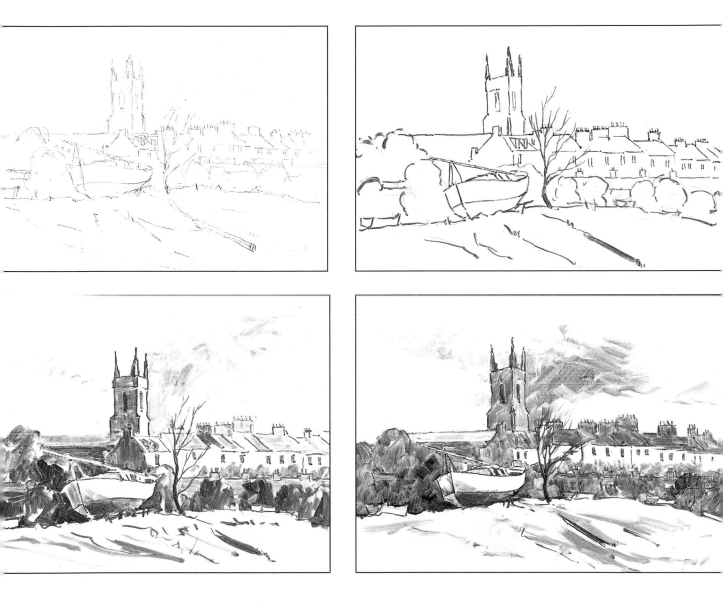

Four ways to start a painting

HOW I SHOWED FOUR WAYS
TO START A PAINTING ON TV

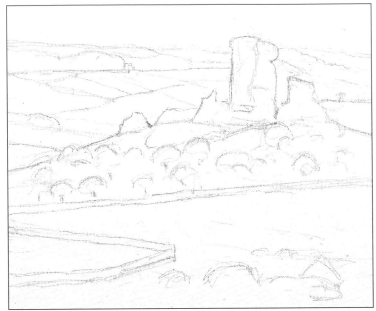

▲ The main areas have been drawn in with a pencil.

▼ The same scene has been drawn in with a brush and
a turpsy mix of Cobalt Blue and Crimson Alizarin.

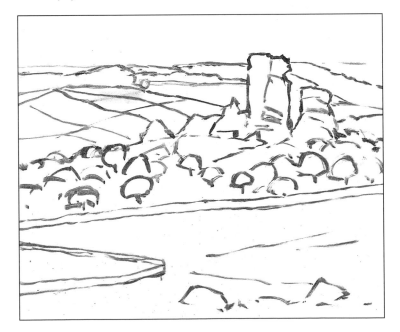

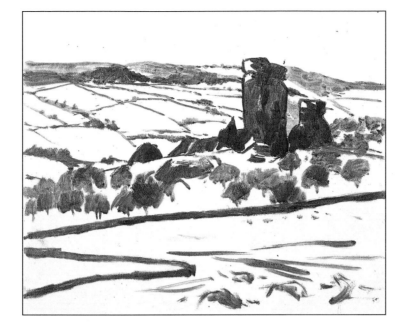

▲ Here the tonal areas have been painted in after the main areas were drawn in with a brush.

▼ The picture has been drawn with a brush, then with colour mixed as a turpsy wash.

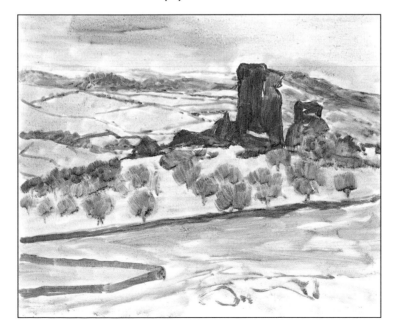

Dartmoor is a fabulous area, full of atmosphere and views. On misty days the landscape is always changing and when there are cloudy, dramatic skies the moors are covered in dark shadows and bright sunlit areas, resulting in tremendous contrasts. But the day we arrived there for filming the sun was out and no clouds or mist were in sight! Fortunately for us, Vixen Tor was almost silhouetted against the bright sky and distant landscape, so it still made a dramatic scene to paint.

After drawing in, I started to paint the sky down to the hills. For a clear sky like this I usually mix Titanium White, Cobalt Blue and a touch of Crimson Alizarin. As I progressed to the horizon I added more Crimson Alizarin to the mix and finally a little Yellow Ochre. I used what was left of the same mix and added more Cobalt Blue for the darker area of the hills, and more Yellow Ochre and Titanium White for lighter colour fields and so on. Then I used Cadmium Yellow, Yellow Ochre, Viridian, Cobalt Blue, a touch of Crimson Alizarin and Titanium White for the different greens in the painting. I am sure that if you have practised mixing greens in the way that I showed you on page 24, you won't have any problems with a painting like this.

I made the Tor a little taller than it really was to give more drama to the painting. This is where your 'artistic licence' comes in! But don't overdo recreating nature or you will end up with some very strange paintings. I put some 'modelling' into the dark rocks with the help of some dull highlights, to give subtle shape and form to them. The tree trunks helped to stabilise the trees. I left the foreground field painted very simply.

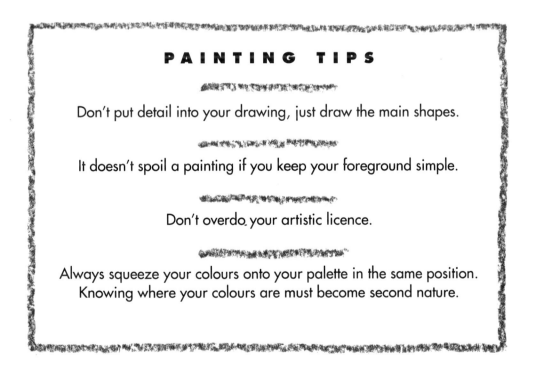

PAINTING TIPS

Don't put detail into your drawing, just draw the main shapes.

It doesn't spoil a painting if you keep your foreground simple.

Don't overdo your artistic licence.

Always squeeze your colours onto your palette in the same position.
Knowing where your colours are must become second nature.

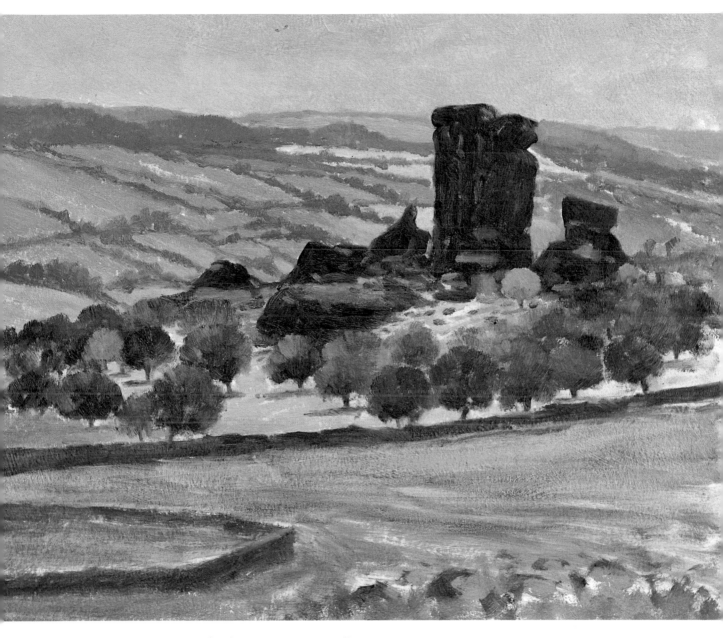

Primed Whatman paper 200 lb Not, 25 × 30 cm (10 × 12 in)

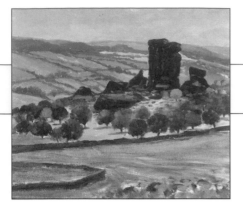

▶ Don't go for detail or try to copy every tree and hedge in a scene. Instead go for the overall shape and mass of things.

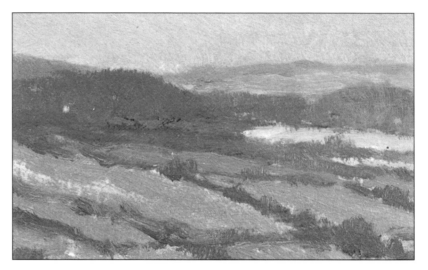

▶ I painted in the trunks and the shadows with a small brush. These brush strokes helped to stabilise the trees.

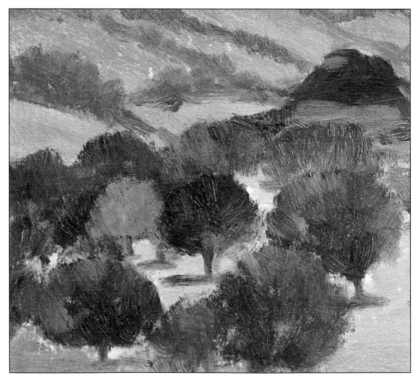

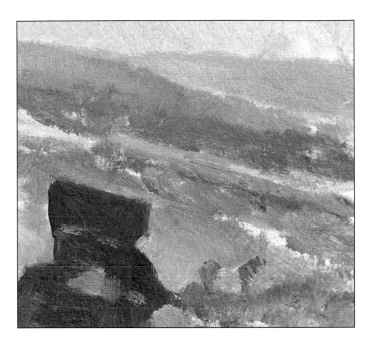

▲ The hills behind the rocks were cooler (I added more Cobalt Blue) than the foreground greens to make them recede into the distance.

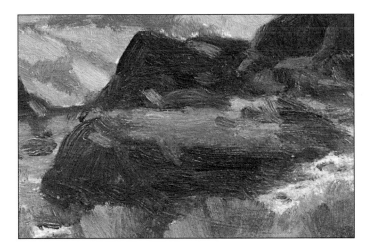

▲ Notice the modelling I put into the rocks. I painted dull highlights on them, using single brush strokes.

► Look at the contrast of the rocks against the background – dark against light. I made the main rocks of Vixen Tor a little taller than real life to give them more drama. Experience will help you to know when and what you can alter.

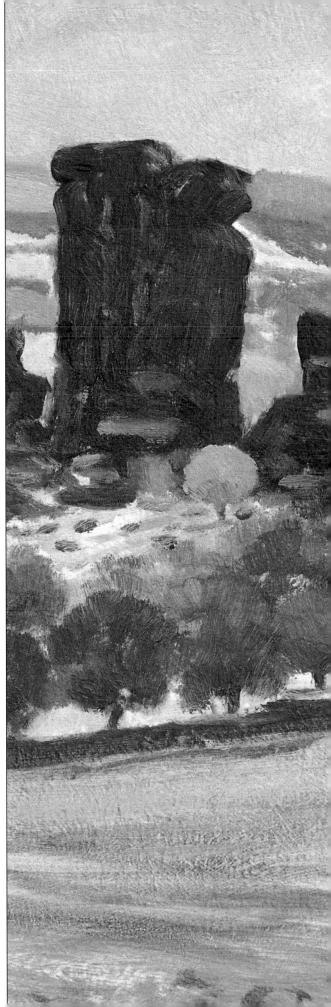

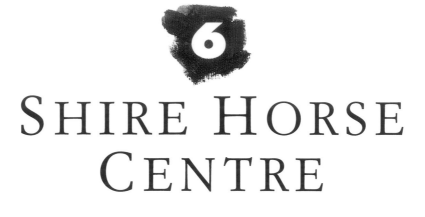

SHIRE HORSE CENTRE

SKETCHING HORSES

If you like shire horses, then the place to see them is the National Shire Horse Centre at Yealmpton in Devon. When we went to film there we had a fabulous day out.

For the pencil sketch on page 51 and the oil sketch on pages 52 and 53, the horses were kept standing in roughly one place by a groom. It had to be this way as, once the cameras were positioned on me and the horses and I began to draw, we couldn't start chasing after them if they decided to wander off!

When I am out sketching animals it usually takes me 15 to 20 minutes to get into the right frame of mind. At first I find that because they move my brain can't cope. You've usually just started drawing when the animal suddenly turns or walks away, and you have to start again or wait until it returns to its original position. I find these first sketches hard work, but after a few I always start to slip into an 'animal drawing mood' and I really enjoy the next hour of sketching. However, after that, my brain usually seizes up once more and, if I'm not careful, my sketches begin to suffer, too. But if I take a ten minute break, I'm soon back in business and happily sketching away again.

When you are sketching horses from life, don't expect to be able to put much detail into your work. The object is to sketch the animal, the way it is standing, its shape, proportions and so on. If its harness is on, that will be part of the sketch, but if you want any detail you will have to work it separately. For instance, if you wanted to work out how to draw the horse's eye, you would only sketch the eye and its immediate surroundings. The same applies to the nostrils, ears, different parts of the harness and so on. You would be extremely lucky to get all this detail into one drawing while the horse stayed in one place.

One very important point to remember here is that you are sketching horses in order to observe and learn about them, not to create a masterpiece. Therefore, if a sketch is started and the horse moves away, don't worry. Simply start another sketch with the horse in its new position, or try a different horse. That's why three of my sketches on the opposite page are parts of and not complete horses. I was lucky with the one *below right* – it kept still!

OPPOSITE AND OVERLEAF **2B pencil on cartridge drawing paper, 20 × 28 cm (8 × 11 in) sketch pad.**

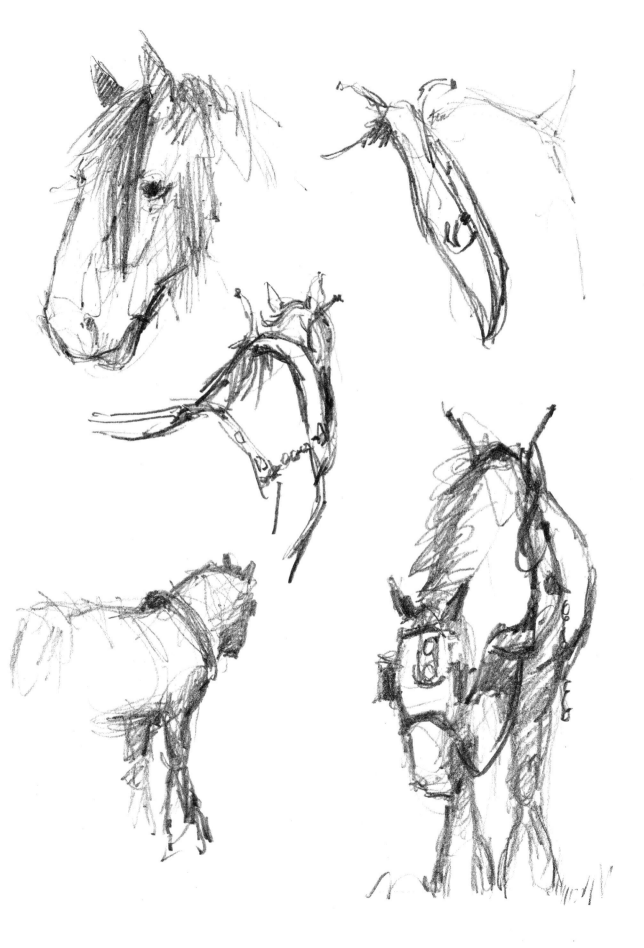

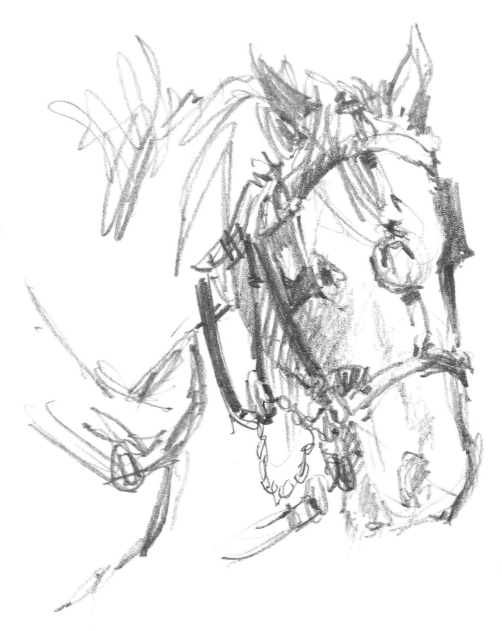

I did the sketches on page 49 and the one above prior to being filmed. These were my 'warming up' sketches and so, by the time the TV crew were ready for me, I was ready, too.

I sketched on camera for about an hour but I did still have some worrying moments. I started to draw one of the horses and it wasn't very good. It gave me one of those sinking feelings when you're sure you'll never be able to draw a horse again! But that's what happens when you draw animals, so if you ever feel this way, don't be put off – *persevere*. It can be hard at first but it's well worth all the effort.

When I am sketching a horse, I usually leave my pencil on the paper most of the time and just move it with a light pressure from place to place. This helps to bring movement and shape into the sketch, so that it doesn't end up looking like an outline drawing. I also add shading with my 2B pencil to give tone and form. The object of sketching animals, apart from enjoying it, is to fill your visual memory with information and, of course, you will always have these pencil sketches from which to work later on.

I did the sketch on the opposite page under camera for the television programme. The horse

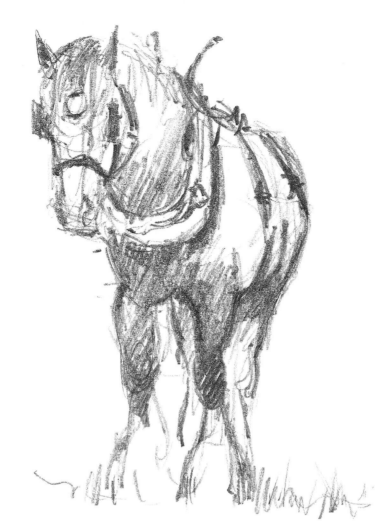

PAINTING TIP

Don't be delicate with your pencil. It has a tonal range from black to very light grey. Use these tones to help give dimension to your drawings.

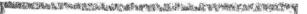

The tonal range of a 2B pencil

kept roughly in one place most of the time, but he couldn't make up his mind whether to keep his head up or down. Naturally it was hard to decide which way to draw it. Still, I made my decision and had to stick to it!

If you have a camera, do take it with you when you go out to sketch horses. Photograph the horses that you are sketching, trying to capture them in the same positions if you can. If you study these photos at home, they will help you greatly with your painting. Of course, there are no short cuts to drawing horses. Although a camera will help, try whenever possible to work from real life. The most important thing is to practise. Remember, with practice comes knowledge and therefore speed – and being able to work fast is definitely a bonus when drawing or painting animals!

I painted the horses, *right*, with a thin turpsy wash after drawing them first with an HB pencil on primed Whatman paper. The drawing was no different from the ones I did in my sketchbook, except that I didn't put any shading in with a pencil. I find that when I paint in this way, which is almost like watercolour painting, I can work more quickly. Once I have the whole sketch painted in, if the horses are still there, I go over it with thicker, opaque paint, as I would on a landscape. With this way of painting, as I mentioned earlier, use more turpentine to thin the paint. This makes it more transparent and lets the underpainting or ground show through. To make areas darker or stronger in colour, use less turpentine and more paint.

If you are lucky enough to be able to paint horses from life like this, then you will certainly progress. Whether you sketch with pencil or paint, the object is always to observe and learn. You may have some half-finished sketches and you will experience both bad and good days. I am no exception! But that is all part of sketching animals and very enjoyable it is, too.

PAINTING TIPS

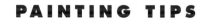

Expect to sketch for up to 20 minutes before you get some acceptable sketches of moving animals.

If you have started sketching and your horse moves away, don't lose your temper – start again!

If you add plenty of turpentine to your paint while sketching, you will find it easier to work quickly. Then use thicker paint over it, or leave it as it is if you prefer.

Primed Whatman paper, 200 lb Not,
25 × 30 cm (10 × 12 in)

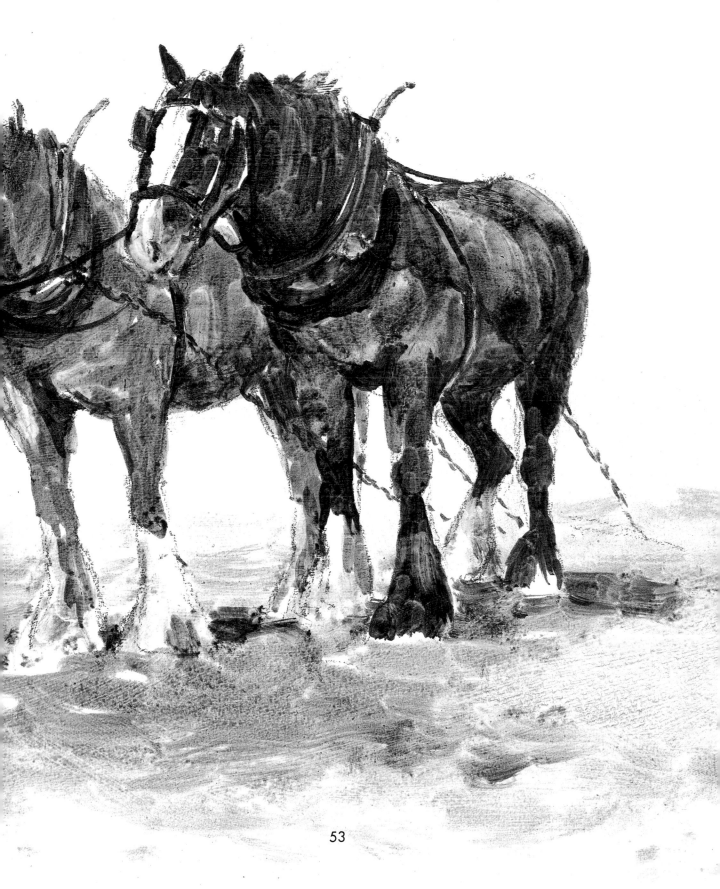

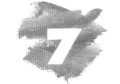

STUDIO

WORKING FROM PHOTOGRAPHS

Students are always asking me, 'Is it all right to paint from photographs?' Well, it is – provided that you observe a few golden rules!

Use a photograph as a reference or starting point to give you inspiration but *never use photos as your only guide to drawing or painting*. You must also work from nature and from objects around you in your home. Also, don't try to copy a photograph slavishly. If you do, your painting won't look good. Finally, wherever possible, use photographs that you have taken yourself. This will help you to remember the mood of the day and many other little things that will then enable you to re-create the scene in paint.

When you look at your photograph, don't just look at the whole picture. See if you could make more than one painting from it. You may find that the whole photograph wouldn't make a good painting, but a section of it would. Try cutting a square hole into a piece of cartridge paper, 4×5 cm ($1^1/2 \times 2$ in), laying it on the photo, and moving it around like a view finder. I am sure you will see some exciting compositions.

If you look at the photograph, *above right*, you will see that I have found three other 'pictures' that could make paintings.

The photograph, *below right*, is dark and not a good photograph, but then I'm not a professional photographer! However, the centre section of it would make a good painting.

Photographs are a useful aid to artists so do use them and don't worry about it. But don't forget to work from nature, too!

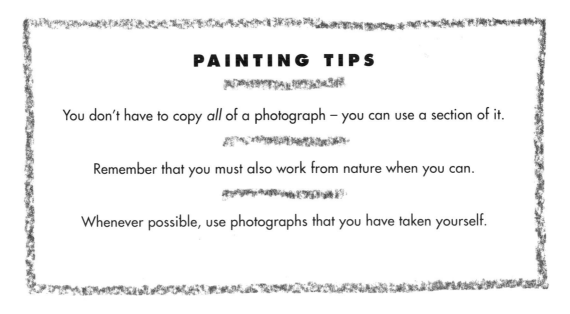

PAINTING TIPS

You don't have to copy *all* of a photograph – you can use a section of it.

Remember that you must also work from nature when you can.

Whenever possible, use photographs that you have taken yourself.

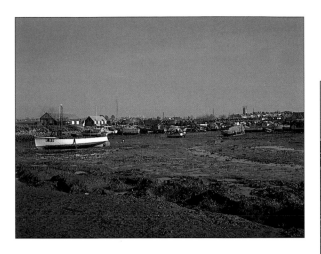

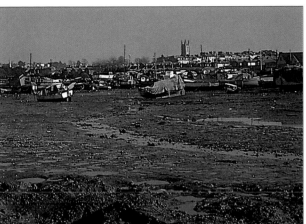

◀ This photograph could make three different paintings.

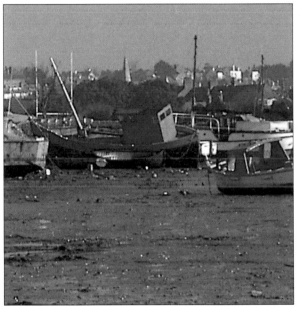

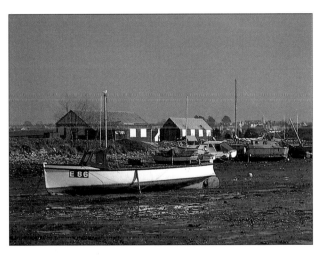

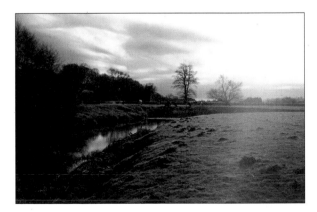

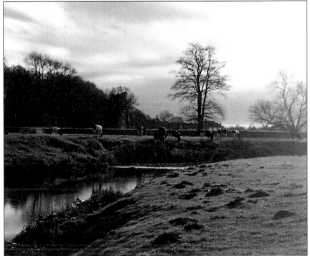

▲ This isn't a good photograph but the section, *right*, would make a painting.

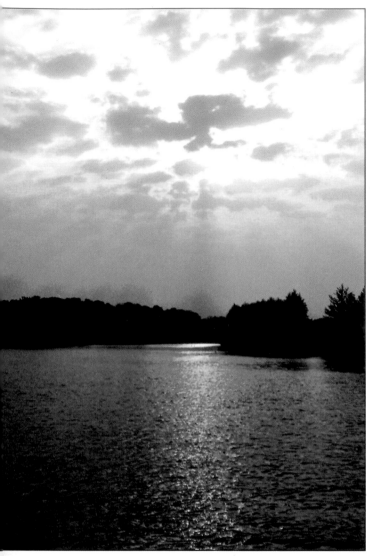

PAINTING SKIES

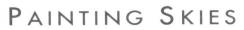

The photograph, *below left*, is a fabulous one of an evening sky with the clouds in perspective to the horizon. You don't get many skies as distinct as this. Unfortunately, for this reason, it wouldn't make a good painting. Although we can accept the unique positions of the clouds in the photograph, they would look contrived in a painting. So if you take a great photograph, it doesn't mean that it will make a great painting. Experience will guide you in this.

In contrast, the photograph of the evening sky, *left*, is perfect for painting. There is nothing exaggerated about it. When I used this to demonstrate how to paint skies from a photograph for the television series, I decided not to put in all the water. I don't like the silhouette of the trees, which is something you get in a photograph taken into the sun but, for this exercise, they are helpful because they show contrast with the sky and, of course, give it scale.

◄ This photograph is perfect for painting – there is nothing exaggerated about it.

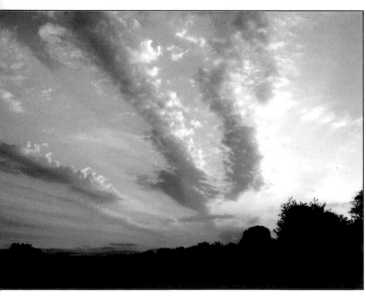

◄ A fabulous photo but the clouds would look false in a painting.

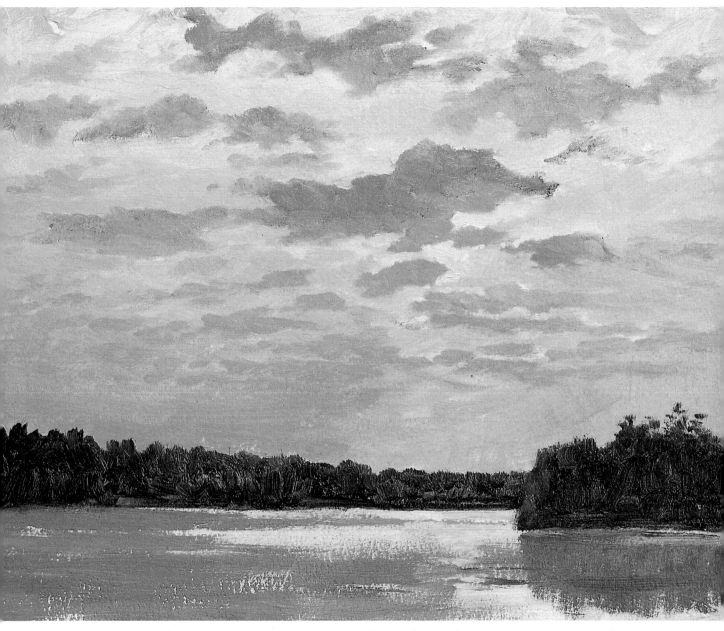

Primed Whatman paper 200 lb Not with a Yellow Ochre wash, 25 × 30 cm (10 × 12 in)

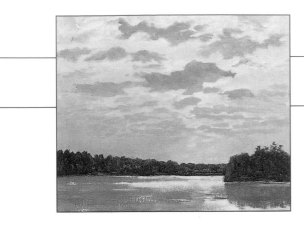

◄ I made the clouds softer and less distinct nearer the horizon to show distance

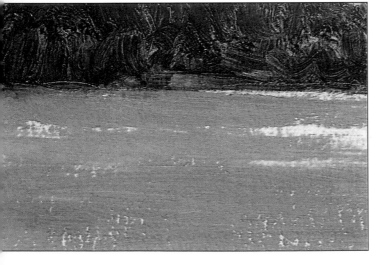

◄ The water was painted with the same colours as the clouds.

► I used thicker paint to put in the sunlit highlights on the clouds. There is very little 'blue' sky in the painting. The photograph was taken in the evening and the sky had turned into a delicate pale mauve, spreading into a pinky-yellow orange. I achieved these colours by mixing Titanium White with a little Cobalt Blue, then adding a little Crimson Alizarin, then Yellow Ochre and more Crimson Alizarin as I worked from the top to the bottom of the sky. I then added a little Cobalt Blue on the left of the sky at the horizon.

58

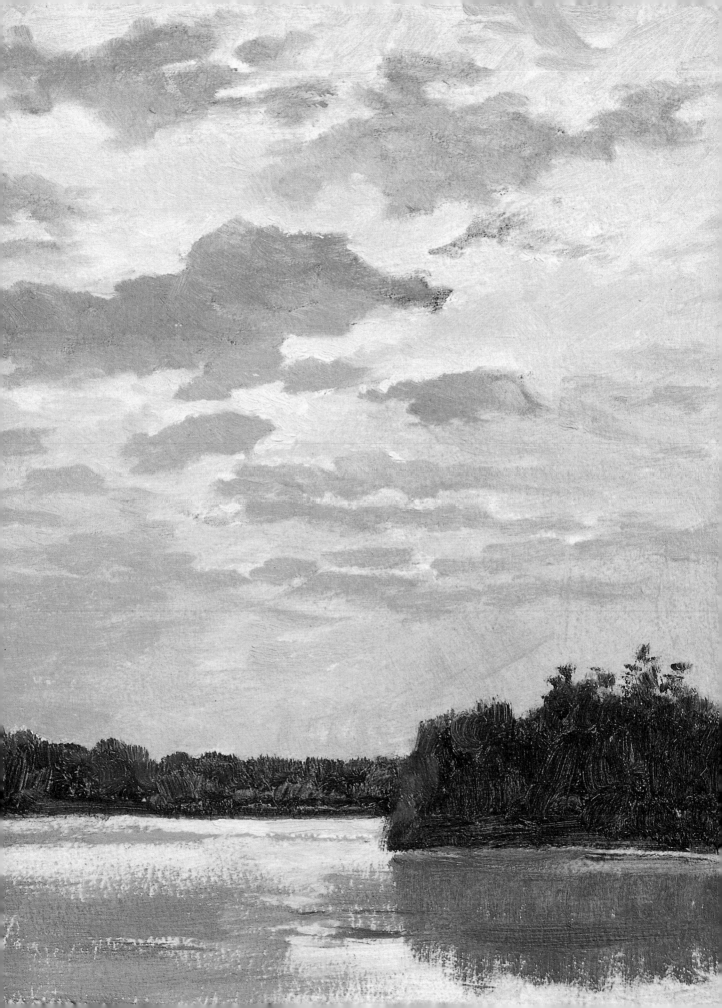

PAINTING REFLECTIONS

Water has always been one of my favourite subjects to paint, but some people do find it difficult. The most important rule to remember is to keep it as simple as you can. Sometimes just one brush stroke can give the effect of water but at other times you need to paint in quite a lot of reflection to give the same impression. Reflections are a very important factor in making water look 'watery'. Always try to reflect something into your water, even in a small puddle across a country path. A reflection in a painting immediately tells the onlooker that it's water even if it isn't painted very well.

In the illustrations *below*, the simplest way to show a reflection is shown on the left. It is a post standing in still, clear water. In the centre, I have used the same post, but the water is moving. This time I have broken the reflection to give the impression of moving water. The water is represented only by the white canvas and yet, because of the reflection, this gives the impression of water.

If an object leans to the left, the reflection is slanted to the right, and vice versa. Look at the post on the right, which is leaning to the left with its reflection slanted to the right. Incidentally, I used blue paint for the water this time and then painted the reflection over the wet paint. You will need to practise painting wet over wet with oil paint, especially working

outside when the paint will not dry during your painting session. You need a very light but firm brush stroke to do this. If you practise on some spare sketching paper you will soon be able to do it. Don't expect to get a very clean, crisp edge every time, because it simply won't happen. Your paint will merge together in places but it doesn't matter. It's all part of the lovely character of an oil painting. In my book *Alwyn Crawshaw's Oil Painting Course* I go into how to paint water in greater detail.

The painting on the opposite page is a good example of how to portray a complicated reflection of buildings in a simplified way. In fact, the whole area of water is a reflection of the houses above. I didn't bother to put much work into the houses or boats because the object was to show you the water and reflection.

You can see how simple the reflection is. It is a copy of the houses on the shore and, of course, the boats. One other important fact is that the reflected colours are all a little darker in tone than the real-life houses. You can use this as a general rule of thumb when you are painting any reflections.

Start with all the dark reflections first, i.e. the windows, shadows on the buildings; then work in the reflections of the buildings. The water I painted on the sky picture on the previous page was done in a much simpler way, but it has a reflection of the trees, and this helps it to look like water. Look carefully at some of your photographs of water, work out how you would paint them and see why the water looks like water. Analyse it and then practise painting it.

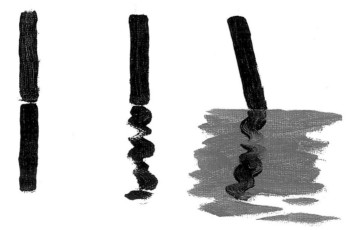

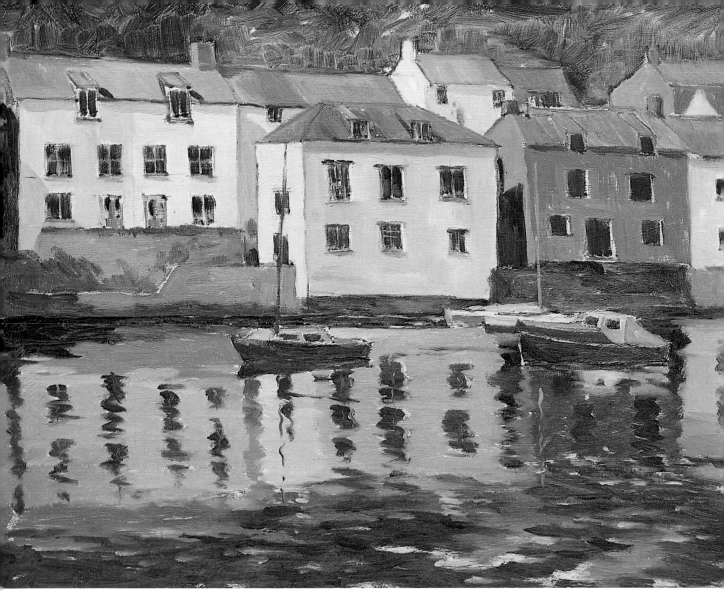

Primed hardboard with a Yellow Ochre wash, 25 × 30 cm (10 × 12 in)

PAINTING TIPS

A painted reflection helps to give the impression of water.

Reflections of objects are usually a little darker than the actual objects.

If the surface of the water is rippling or disturbed, break up the reflected image. This helps to create the illusion of movement on the water. Don't overwork water – it can be painted very simply to get good results.

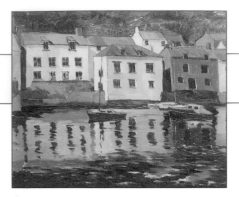

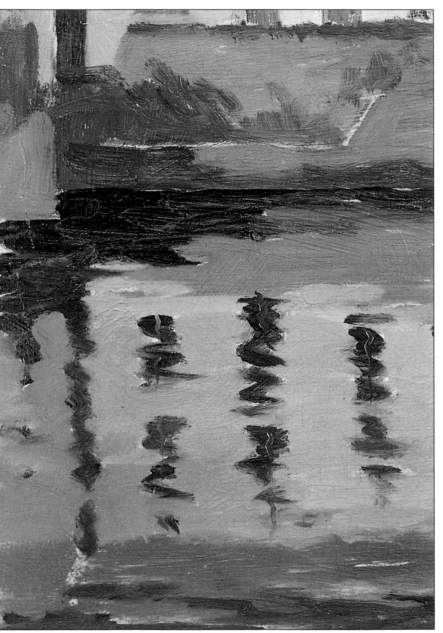

◄ The dark reflections were painted in first, then the houses.

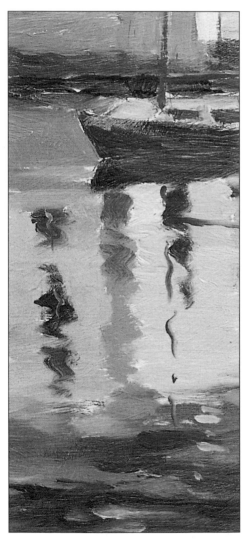

▲ The light reflection was painted and then, with my rigger brush, I painted in the mast reflection.

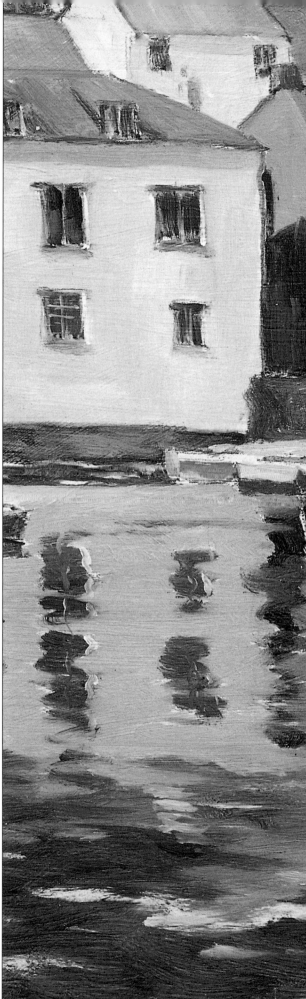

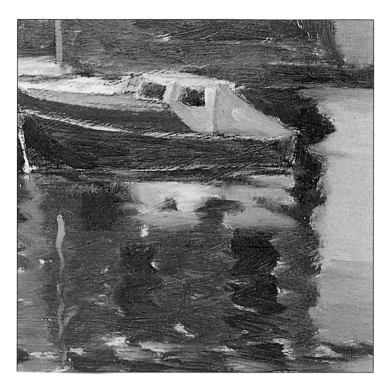

▲ The contrast in the reflection between the building and the windows is not as strong as in real life. If it had been, it would have looked wrong. The reflection of the mast was painted over afterwards with my rigger brush.

► I added the highlights of the window frames after I painted in the windows and walls. Notice how freely I painted these to give the impression of moving water.

8

OTTERY ST MARY

PAINTING PEOPLE AND TREES

These trees were painted on canvas board, the same size that they are shown here.

Filming this programme took me right back to my youth, when I used to play cricket for my town in Sussex while I was still at art school. It was a very hot cloudless day, so we chose a position in the shade of some trees and I prepared for an exciting day's painting.

I must admit that I found it very difficult at times to concentrate on the painting, shown on pages 68 and 69, with the match progressing! But before I talk about the cricket painting, I want to show you how to paint trees.

The two trees illustrated, the one on the left which isn't in leaf and the one on the right which is, have both been painted in a simplified way. I always start by painting the trunk, beginning at the bottom and working up the tree in the direction that it grows. Use your B.48 No. 2 brush and then let the brush leave the

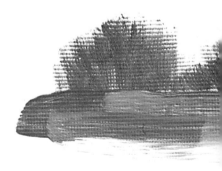

64

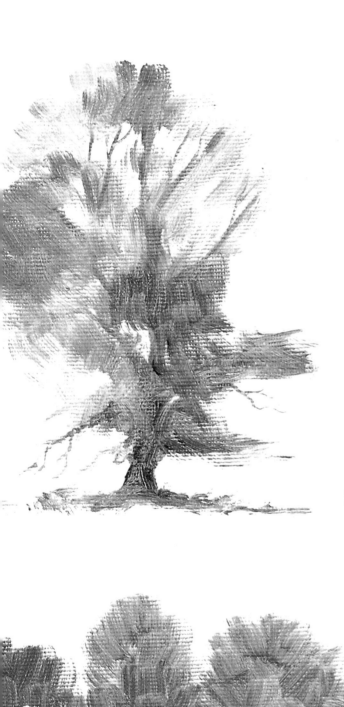

trunk and continue upwards, painting the branches. Use your rigger for the smaller branches. Then with a *dry* turpsy wash, and using your flat brush, drag it over the branches to suggest the very small feathery branches. It doesn't matter if it pulls up some of the already painted branches, as this helps to make the tree look more three-dimensional. You can also paint some back over the top if you like.

A summer tree in leaf is worked in exactly the same way, except that you use thicker paint to paint over the trunk and branches. The fence that I suggested on the left-hand tree is important, as it gives scale to it.

The row of distant trees or bushes below are created by a flat brush, with one brush stroke for the field painted across the bottom of them. This gives the impression that they are just over the brow of a hill. Practise these trees – it's a simple way to get started. As you progress, try using thicker paint and also go outdoors and practise copying real trees

PAINTING TIPS

Don't overwork trees – keep them simple.

With individual trees, leave some 'holes' of sky through the foliage. You can always paint the sky colour back over the tree if you need more sky to show through.

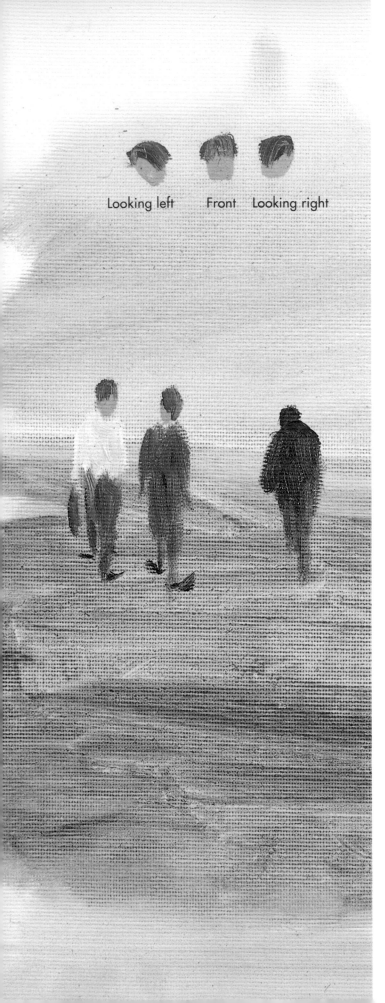

Looking left   Front   Looking right

You can't paint a cricket scene without painting people. Shown *left* is the exercise I did on the TV screen. The pink blobs at the top are faces, and the dark shapes on top of these is their hair. They look very simple, and they are. The one in the middle is a face looking *towards us*. The one on the left is looking to *our left* and the one on the right is looking to *our right*. All this is done with just two brush strokes: first one for the head, then the hair is added with a darker colour. This is simple but very effective.

The heads of the two figures below them are done in just the same way and they look as though they are talking to one another. When painting figures always start with the head then work down the body and legs. Do this in just one brush stroke if the colour is the same, see the figure on the right, or two strokes if the colour changes, see the left-hand figure. This very impressionist treatment is all you need when you put figures into a landscape or harbour scene, where the figures are subordinate to their surroundings. If a figure were to be used close up in a painting as the centre of interest, then it would have to have much more careful work put into it.

Don't put feet on your figures unless they are close up, or where the feet help to suggest the action of the figure, like the cricketers on the right. You can see that the figures on the left look like Charlie Chaplin characters! That's because I added feet to them in the television programme after I had painted the figures, to illustrate that particular point.

I did some pencil sketches of the cricketers while the crew was organising their equipment, and naturally it loosened me up for my painting in exactly the same way as sketching the shire horses had in the previous programme. Figure drawing has the same problems as drawing horses because people move, too. You can always practise sketching people from the TV screen. It's not easy, but it's fun to do.

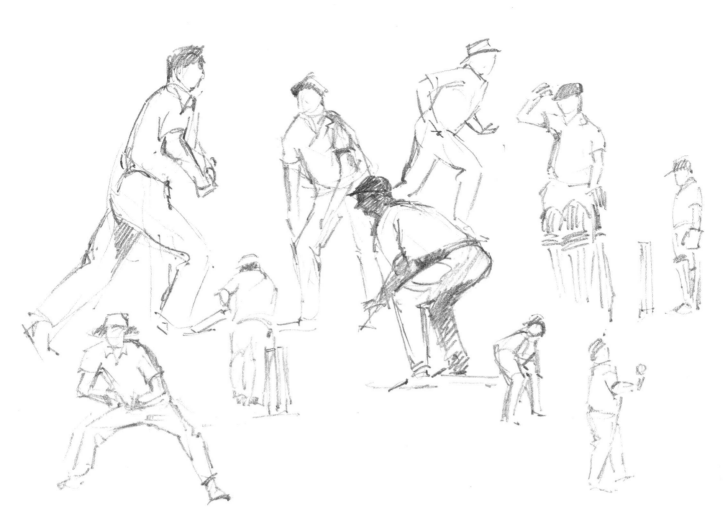

2B pencil on cartridge paper

The painting shown overleaf was the largest one that I did for the series. It was 40 × 60 cm (16 × 24 in) and I did it sitting at an easel, not using my pochade box. I felt later that I could have made the grass a little darker in tone to contrast against the white cricketers. Also the shadow of the trees on the grass in the foreground could have had a little more blue in it. But apart from that I was happy with it.

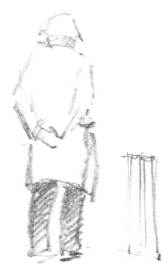

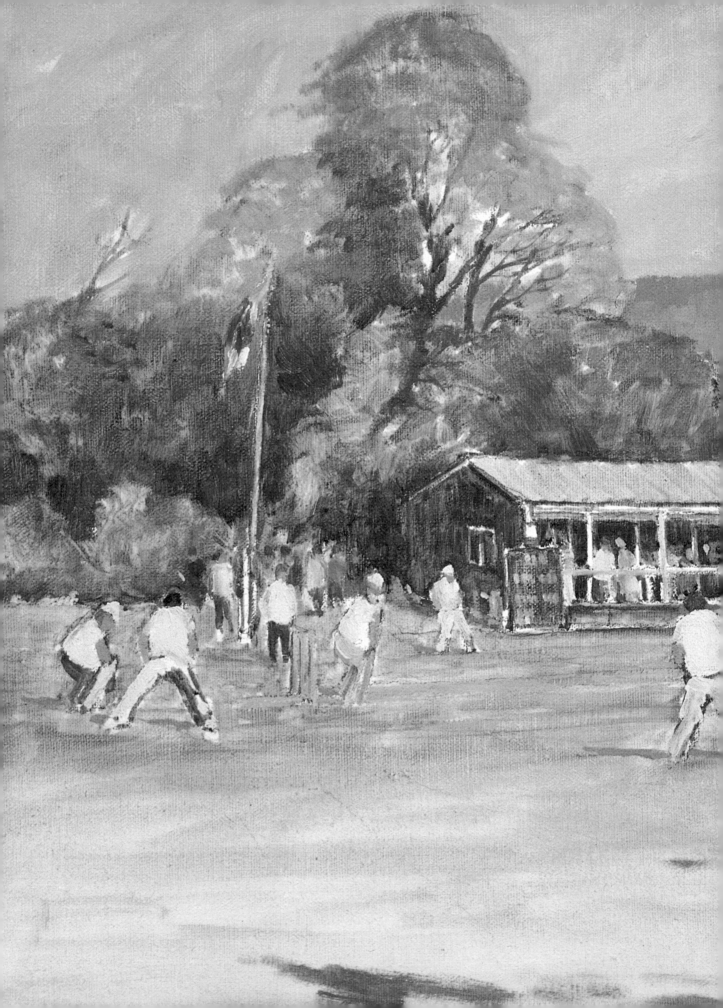

Primed canvas, 40 × 60 cm (16 × 24 in)

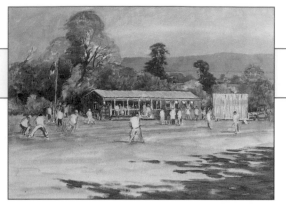

▶ These two cricketers are very strongly defined. Notice how dark the shadows are on their white trousers. Never be afraid to paint dark shadows on white or light objects.

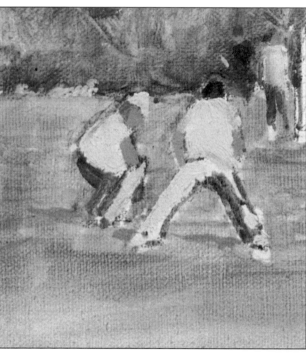

▶ The definition of the close-up cricketer has been achieved by leaving some of the original blue drawing line showing. Also I've used a darker tone on the trousers. The people in the pavilion are painted in cool blueish colours except for the one leaning on the handrail. He has caught the sunlight.

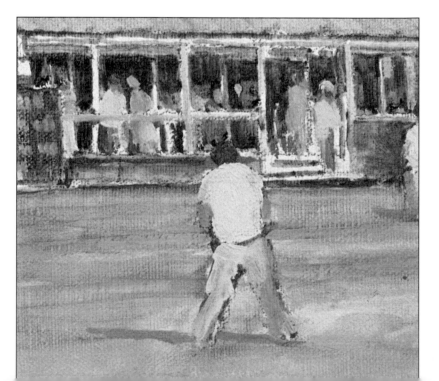

► The flag is important. Apart from adding colour, it also conveys to the onlooker that there is practically no wind. This helps to suggest atmosphere.

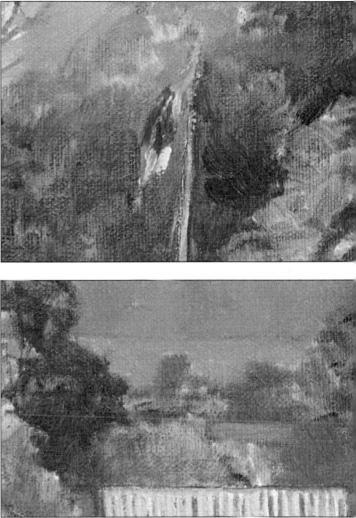

▼ If you look at this detail the important issue here was to make sure that I showed the umpire with his black trousers. I was never completely happy with the batsman – he just wouldn't keep still!

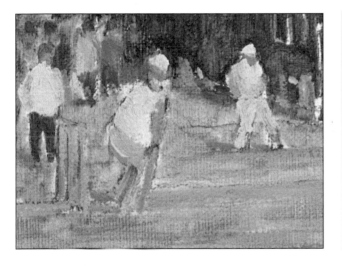

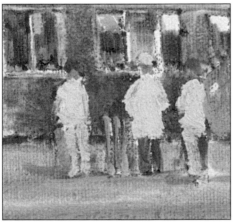

▲ I treated the landscape background very simply. I didn't want to distract attention from the cricketers on the pitch.

◄ Again the umpire was very important. I made sure that I put in his black trousers and also his white coat, which separates him from the players.

CANVASES ON CAMERA

Behind the scenes on location with *Crawshaw Paints Oils*

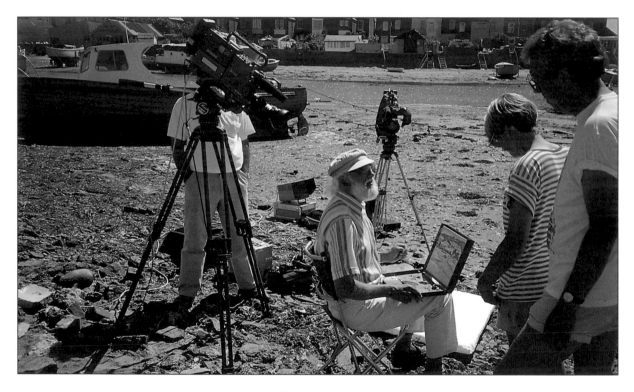

▲ 'No, the tide won't come in, Ingrid.'

Planning a television series has to be done in great detail and this, my third television series, was no exception. Firstly, I had to decide how best to present the programmes and instruct viewers in the basic principles of oil painting while inspiring them as well. Then I needed to find eight suitable locations for the paintings I would do under camera which also fitted in with the teaching principles of each particular programme. It sounds easy but, even with the

whole of Devon and Cornwall at my disposal, this was one of the hardest jobs of all! June and I spent ten very hectic days driving around the countryside looking for views to paint. We decided on twelve locations, giving ourselves four extra as a safety margin.

The following week, David Hare, the producer, and Ingrid Duffell, our director, came down to see them. Naturally they both had their own criteria for a good spot. There had to be

72

space for a camera in front of me – the one to which I would talk – and one behind me – the one that would be filming me while I painted. We couldn't have a noisy location as this would give the sound technician problems. Finally, not only must each scene I paint be a 'pretty' one for the viewers as well as being instructional for my painting, but the view *behind* me which the camera sees had to be as attractive as possible, too. Viewers don't want to look at a brick wall or a rusty old car wreck behind me when I'm talking to them!

Six of the scenes that June and I had chosen were ideal and satisfied everyone. This still left two more to find but eventually these were decided upon too. With so many factors to agree on to make the perfect scene, I'm very surprised we found any!

When we decided on the Exe estuary at Exmouth, the tide was out so the schedule was arranged for me to paint the scene at low tide. However, when we arrived there for filming there was a very strong wind and the spot where

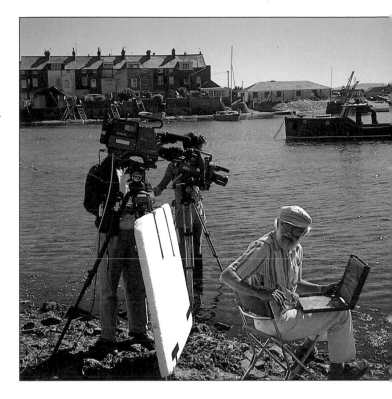

▲ 'All right, I was wrong!'

I had decided to paint from was right in the wind, making it impossible to film. We all had a worrying fifteen minutes as I looked around for another suitable painting spot. I decided to work low down on the estuary mud and stones where the tide came in because this was out of the wind. Ingrid looked at me enquiringly and asked whether the tide would come up to my spot. 'Oh, don't worry, Ingrid,' I said. 'We'll have finished before it reaches here. Look how far away it is now!'

So everything was set up and I started to paint. I know that the tide comes in quickly at Exmouth because the estuary is very flat and I have painted there many times, but I am sure that on this particular day it was trying to break all records! I finished the painting with my feet in the sea, and one of the camera men was nearly up to his knees in water. The last part of the painting did get a little frantic, and I'm sure that Ingrid won't ever believe me again!

Lympstone, also on the Exe estuary, had its

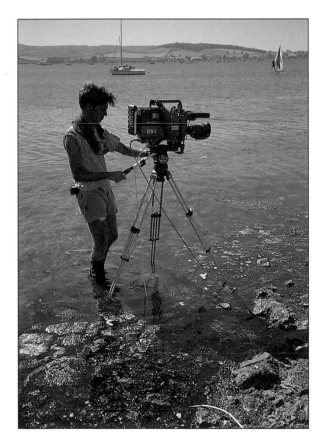

◄ And the tide came in and in...

73

share of 'tide problems', too, but this time they were on dry land. It was a gloriously warm day and it seemed that everyone who had a boat moored there was taking it out that day. I think I was interrupted more times doing this painting than with with any other I have done on camera. However, although I felt a little harassed at times, that painting turned out to be one of my favourites of the series. At one point a crowd of children come from nowhere and surrounded me, so we made this a natural break and I enjoyed chatting to them.

There always seem to be distractions when you are near water. When we filmed at Newton Ferrers, I was sitting on the quayside, well above the water level. The tide was coming in while I painted it and as the sea came alongside me I could see lots of large fish – I believe they were mullet – swimming about. I'm a keen angler and you can imagine how distracting it was to have those fish teasing me while I was painting!

We got far away from distractions when we went to Dartmoor. It was a lovely day again and we seemed to have the moor to ourselves apart from a few sheep, horses and cows.

The National Shire Horse Centre was a very exciting day's filming. There were horses, people, children and lots of noise – almost everything that makes our type of filming tricky. If that wasn't enough, the subject that I was going to paint was a moving object with a mind of its own! This was the one programme location that I was dreading. However, we were looked after very well during the day by the staff of the centre and, despite all the potential problems, everything went smoothly, so you never can tell!

I thoroughly enjoyed making the last programme and painting the cricket match, particularly as it took place in Ottery St Mary, a town where I once lived for several years. The surroundings were beautiful and the weather was

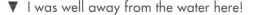

▼ I was well away from the water here!

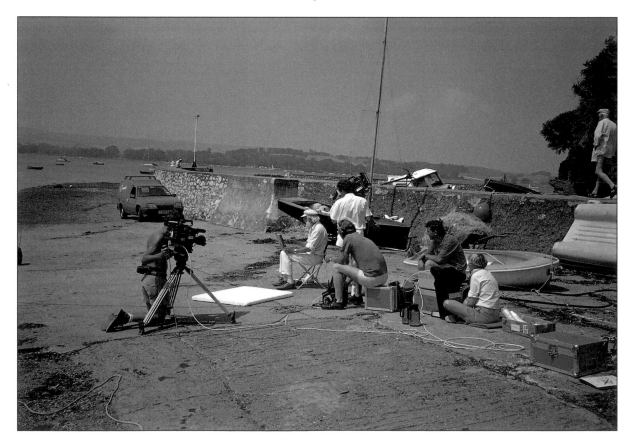

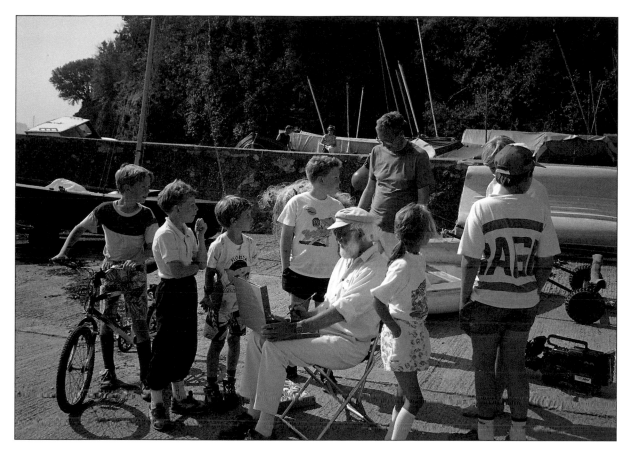

▲ 'Will we be on television, too?'

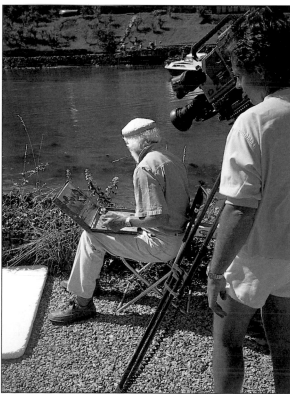

◄ 'Look, there's another one!'

▼ Far away from the madding crowd, water,
boats – and fish.

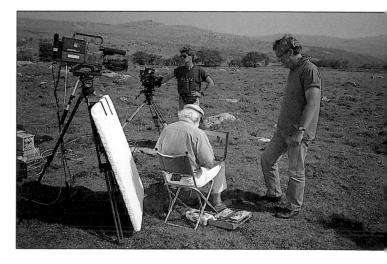

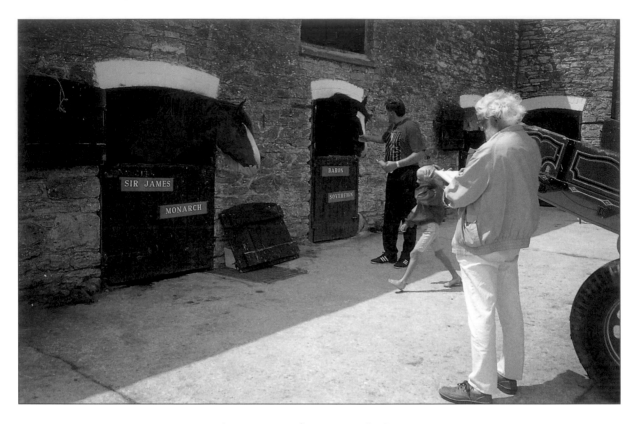

▲ 'I promise this won't take long.'

very hot, with hardly any wind. All in all, it was an idyllic day. The hardest part for me was to concentrate on my painting and not be distracted by the cricket match too much! During the filming of the series there were obviously many incidents that made us laugh or want to tear our hair out. One such occasion that will stay in my mind was at Lympstone when we were filming an establishing shot of me arriving at the quayside and explaining what a lovely place it was. I had to walk down the quay for some distance towards the camera as it filmed me, then stop in front of it and deliver my lines.

We were on our fifth take, having been interrupted by boats being docked and launched and people wandering in front of the camera. An elderly couple couldn't make up their minds whether to go down the quay before or after we had filmed. It was becoming like a comic opera, so Ingrid suggested that they should walk down now, in front of me, so that they would be out of camera shot when I delivered my lines. They

were asked not to look at the camera and to walk straight past it.

At this point I was starting to lose concentration and get my lines jumbled up in my mind. We had two false starts when the couple headed the wrong way first of all and then stopped halfway down the quay the second time. Finally, we were on our way, with me

▼ 'All right, be like that then.'

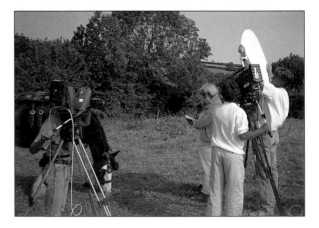

following behind them looking at different views in the harbour. Then, unbelievably, the man – instead of walking past the camera – walked straight up to it and started talking. 'I don't know why you're making a film here. It's much prettier at Henley-on-Thames, where we live,' he said! The only answer to that was *'Cut!'* But at least they had finally passed the camera and we were able to start again.

On the next take, I fluffed my lines – and I wasn't surprised! However, the next one went perfectly and the crew sent up a cheer in unison. We were extremely relieved to get that scene finally in the can – even though I was a nervous wreck by this time!

I hope that this brief glimpse behind the scenes will entertain you. I also hope it will inspire you to find some exciting but less complicated locations in which to work yourself. I should mention that June is always behind the scenes when I am working, helping me in all sorts of artistic ways. However, in one of my other television series, *Crawshaw Paints On Holiday*, June is featured painting under camera alongside me. After her first painting for that series, she said, 'I know what it's like on the *other* side of the camera now!' She had always been concerned about working outside before, but I believe the TV series has helped her overcome her fears.

For those of you who are worried about painting outside where the public can watch you, remember one thing. Even if it's the first time you've ever painted, *they* won't know this. They will simply see you as an artist and probably secretly admire you for working outside in the public eye.

I hope that the television series and this book have brushed away some of the mystery that usually surrounds oil painting and will help to give you the confidence to paint in oils yourself. So, if you are wondering whether to start, take my advice. Have and go and enjoy it. It really is easier than you think – *but don't forget to practise!*

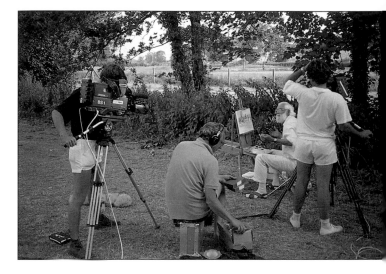

▲ 'Howzat!'

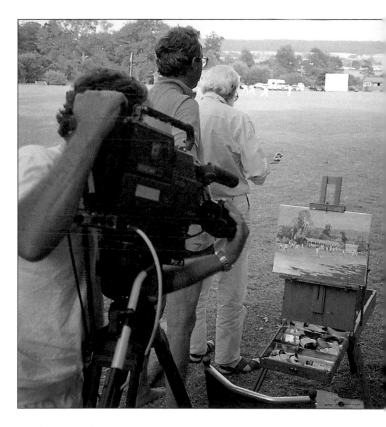

▲ The end of a long and enjoyable day.

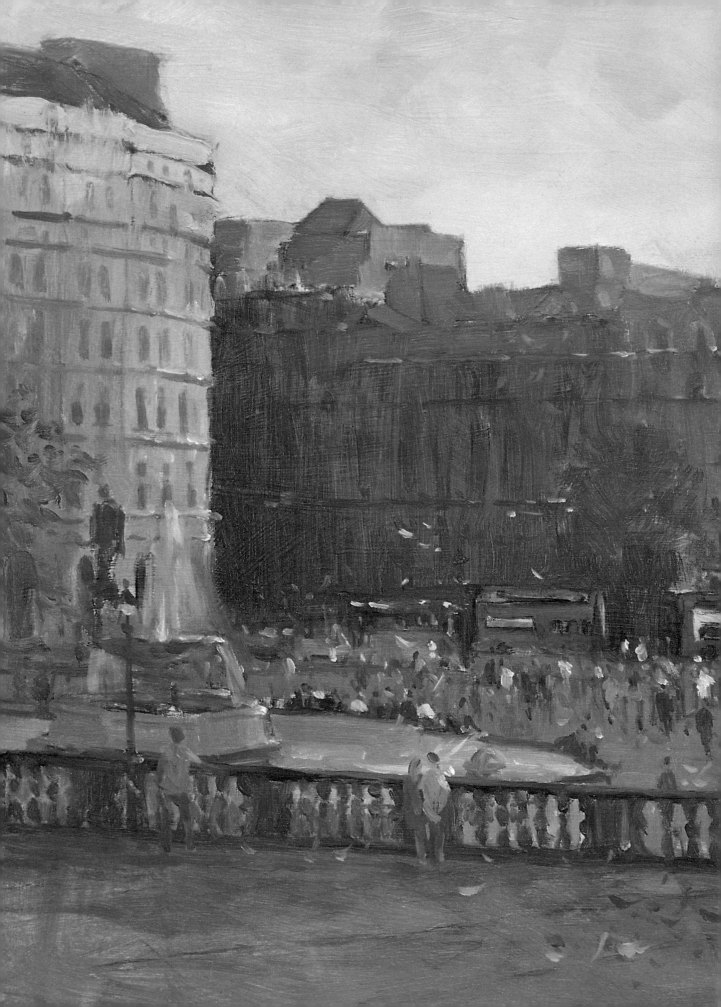

GALLERY

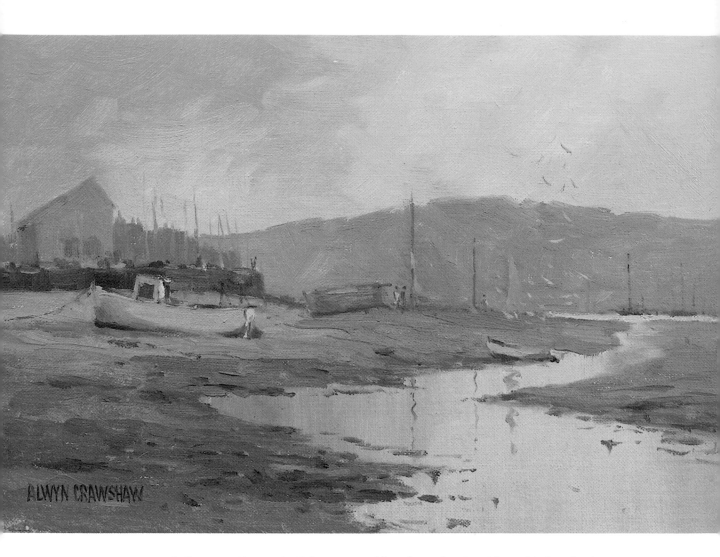

▲ *Evening, Exmouth.* Oil on primed hardboard, 16 × 23 cm (6¹/₂ × 9 in)

◄ *Newton Ferrers, Devon.* Oil on canvas, 40 × 50 cm (16 × 20 in)

PREVIOUS PAGE *Trafalgar Square, London.* Oil on primed hardboard, 30 × 40 cm (12 × 16 in)

► *Low water, looking towards Newton Ferrers Church, Devon.* Oil on canvas, 40 × 50 cm (26 × 20 in)

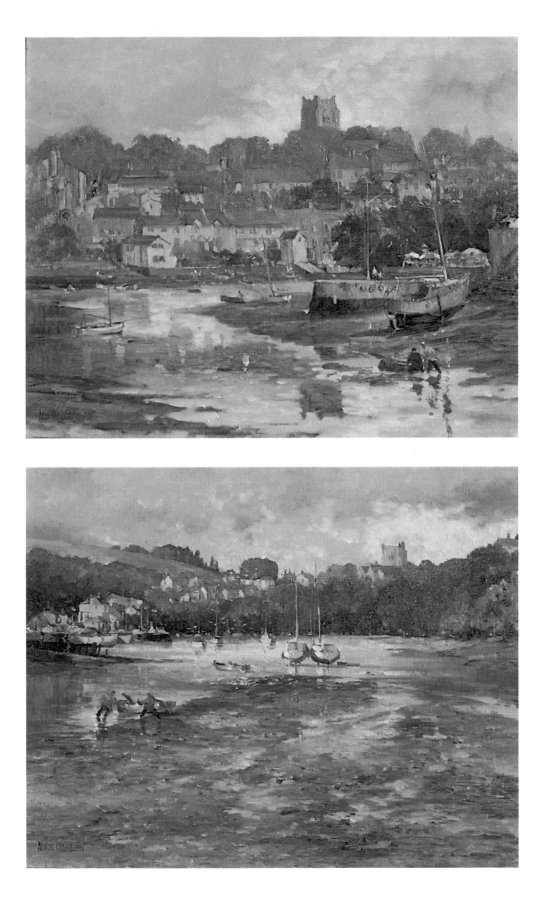

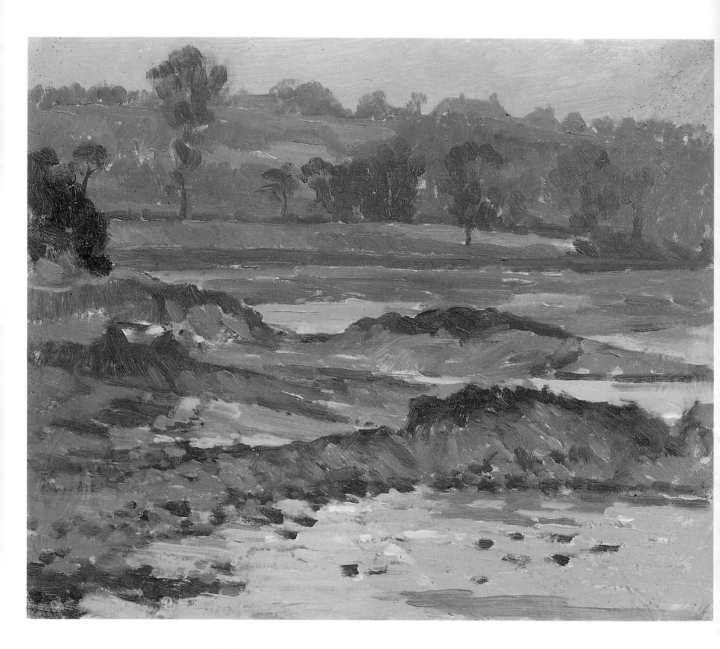

Evening light, Jersey. Oil on primed hardboard, 25 × 30 cm (10 × 12 in)

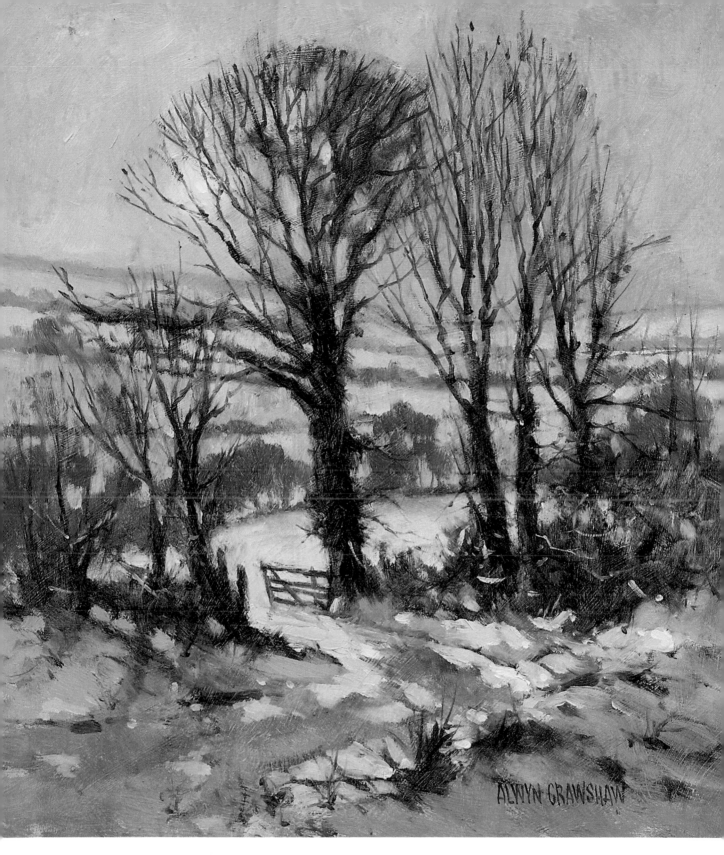

Snow in Wales. Oil on primed hardboard, 30 × 25 cm (12 × 10 in)

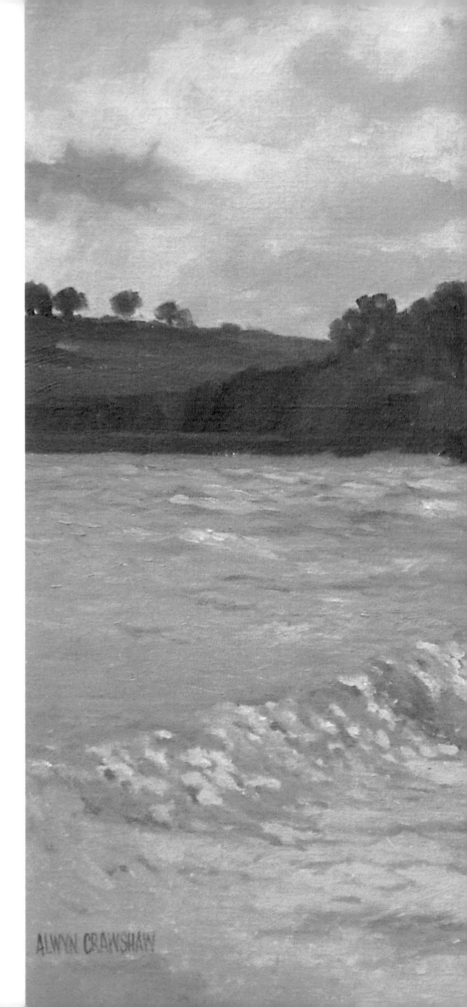

Late evening, Dawlish Beach, Devon. Oil on canvas, 40 × 50 cm (16 × 20 in)

ALWYN CRAWSHAW

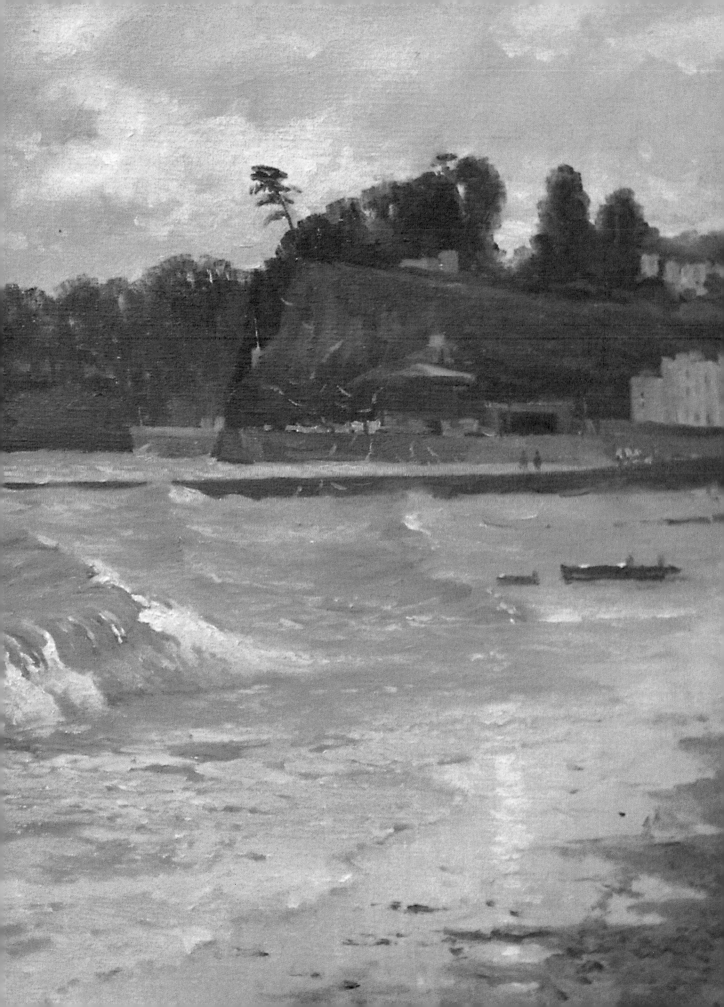

Le Bourg, St Clement, Jersey.
Oil on primed Whatman 200 lb Not,
25 × 30 cm (10 × 12 in)

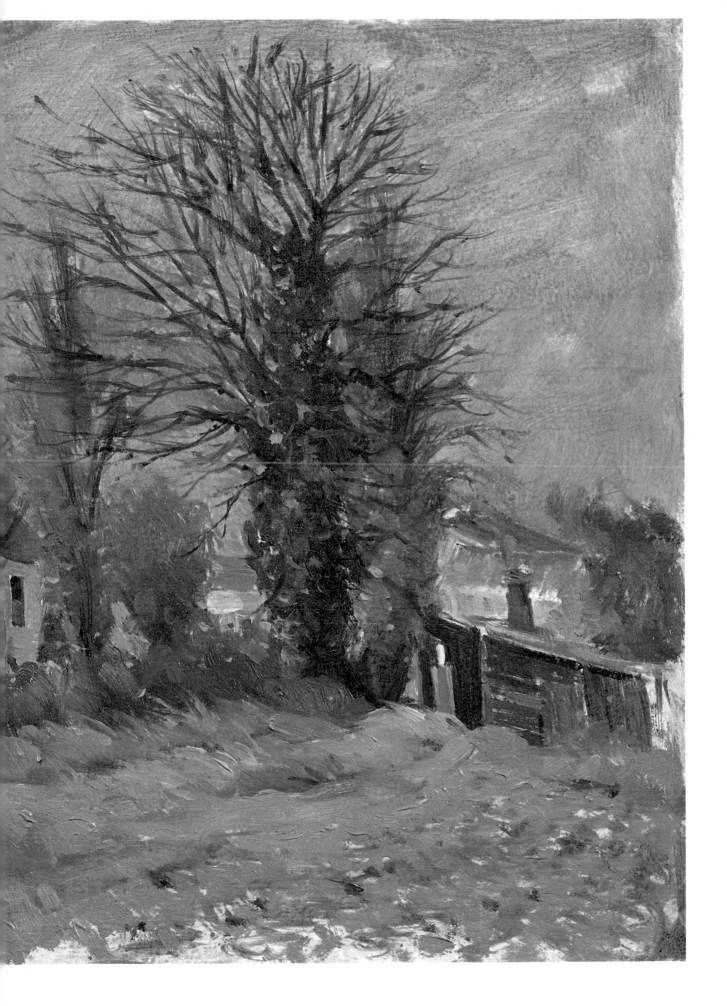

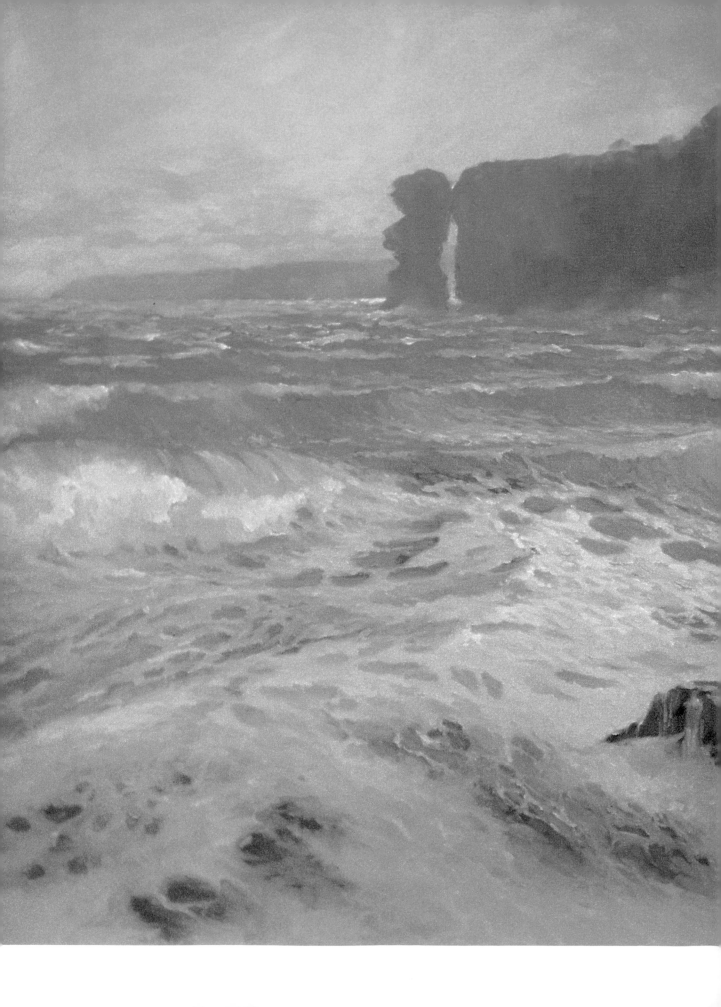

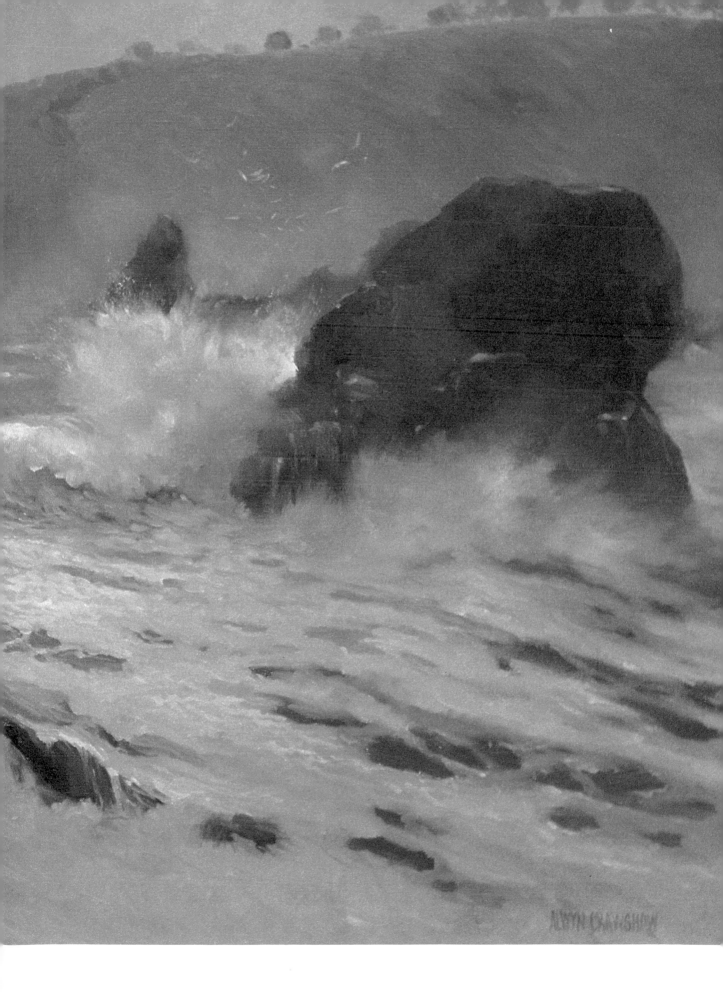

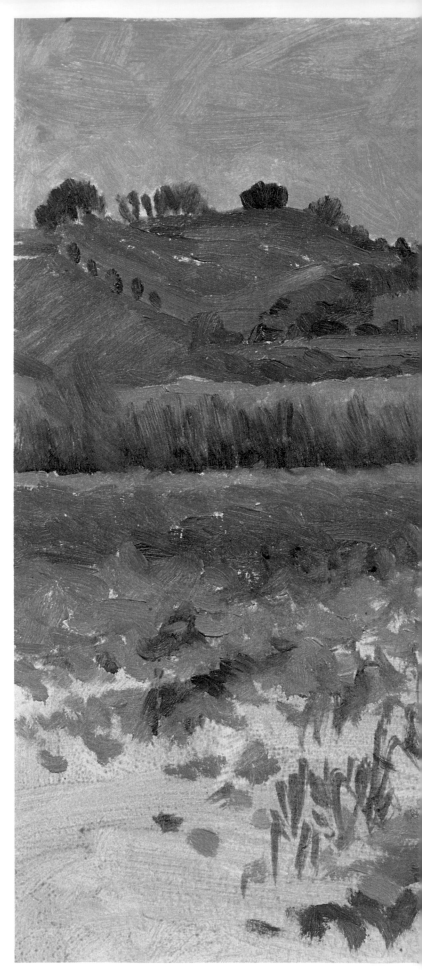

*Looking towards Le Verclut,
Grouville, Jersey.*
Oil on primed Whatman 200 lb Not,
25 × 30 cm (10 × 12 in)

PREVIOUS PAGE *Last sunlight, Dawlish,
Devon.* Oil on canvas,
60 × 90 cm (24 × 36 in)

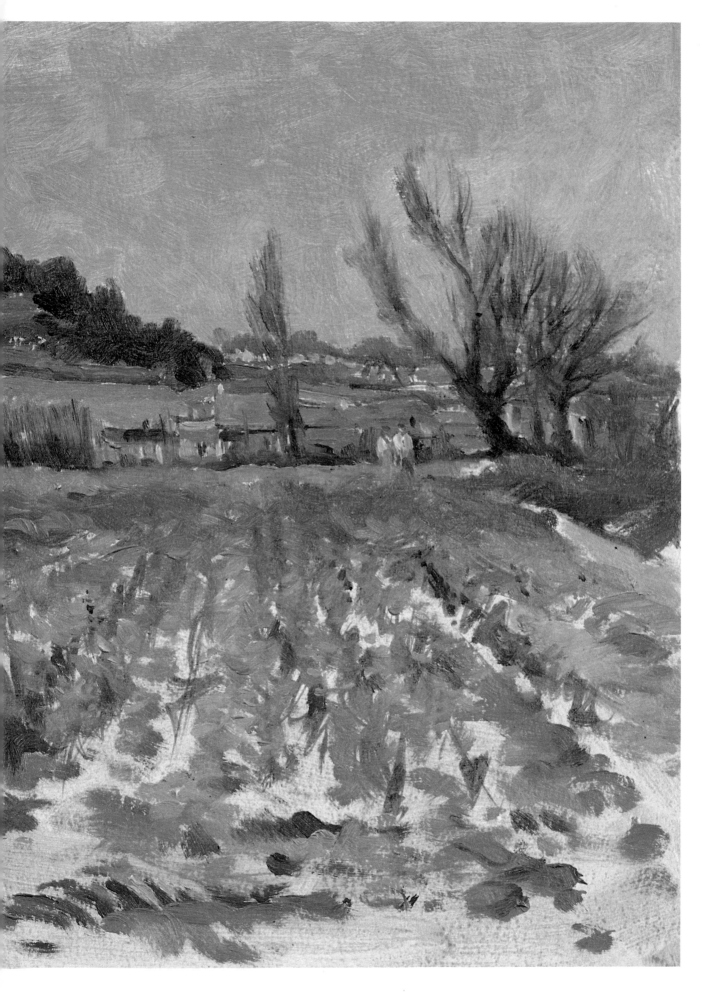

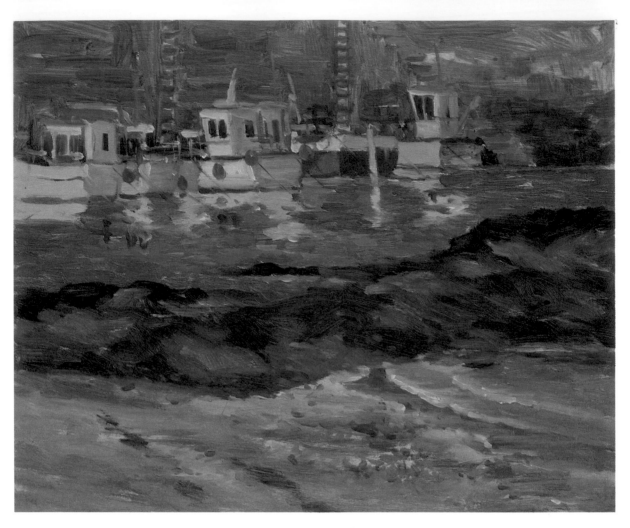

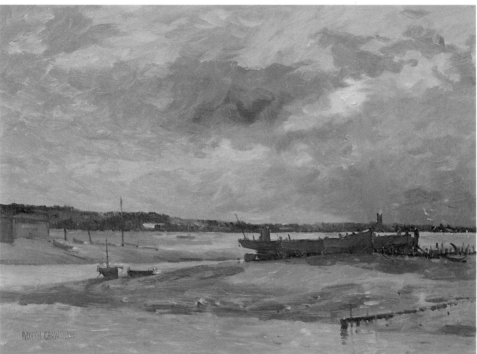

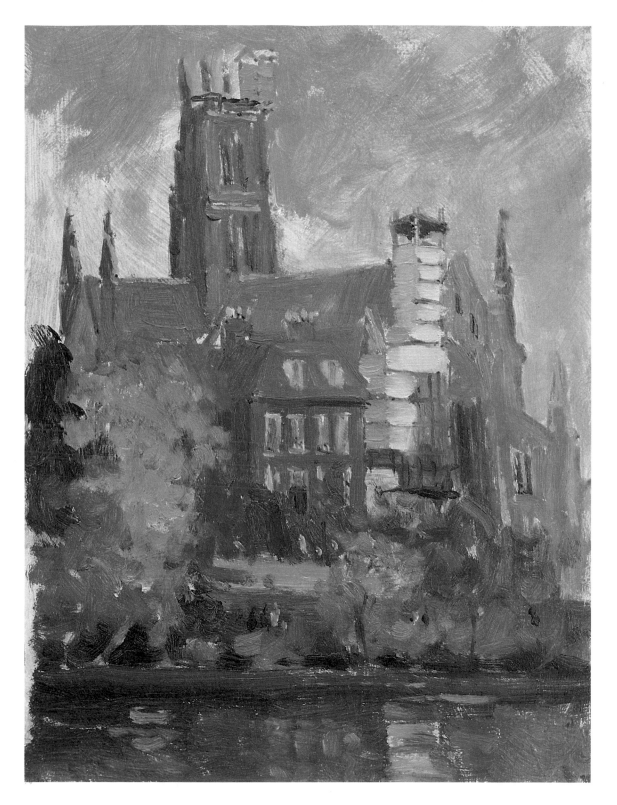

▼ *Rozel Harbour, Jersey.* Oil on primed
hardboard, 25 × 30 cm (10 × 12 in)

▲ *Worcester Cathedral.*
Oil on primed hardboard,
20 × 15 cm (8 × 6 in)

◄ *Topsham, Devon.* Oil on primed
hardboard, 30 × 40 cm (12 × 16 in)

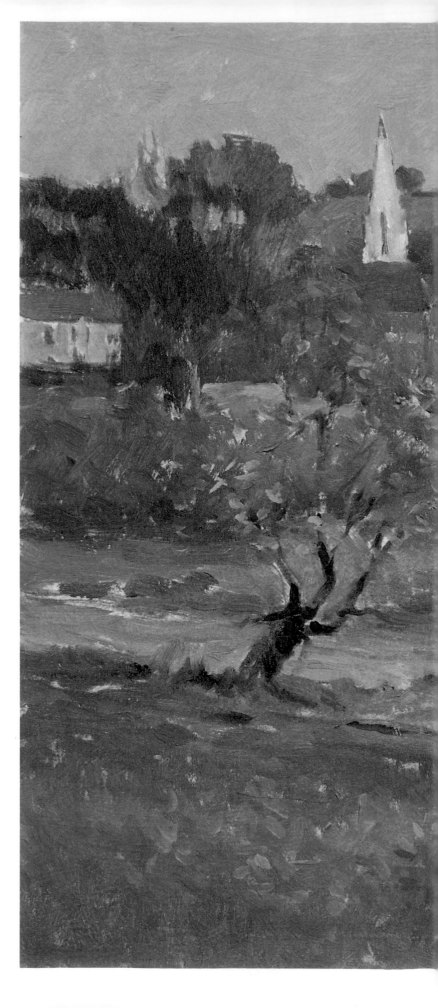

Late afternoon light, Grouville Church, Jersey. Oil on primed Whatman 200 lb Not, 25 × 30 cm (10 × 12 in)

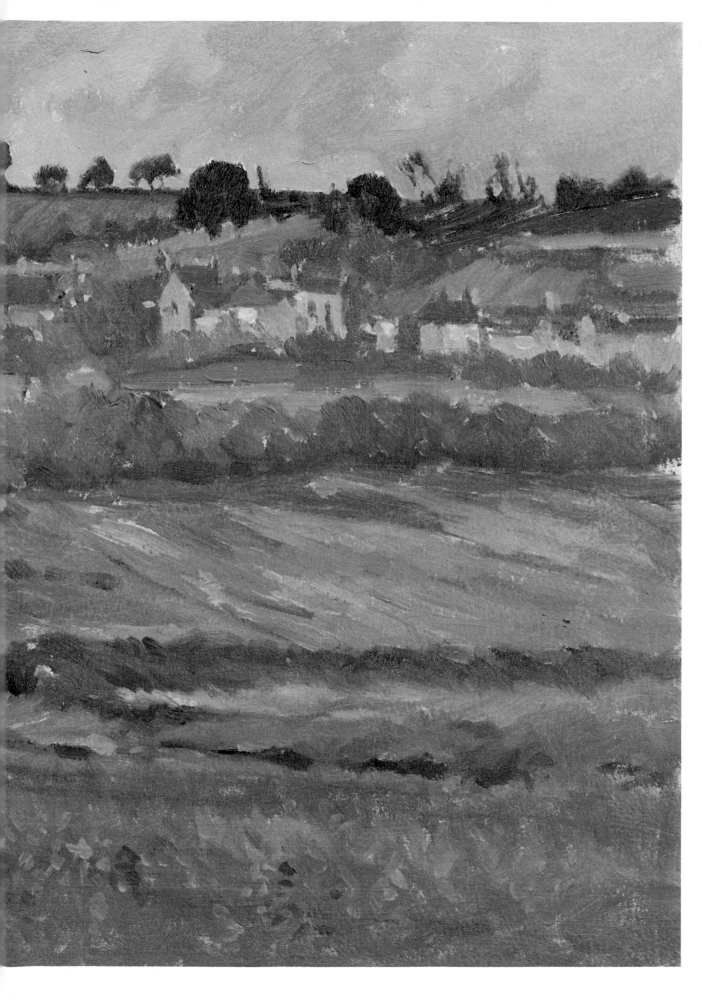

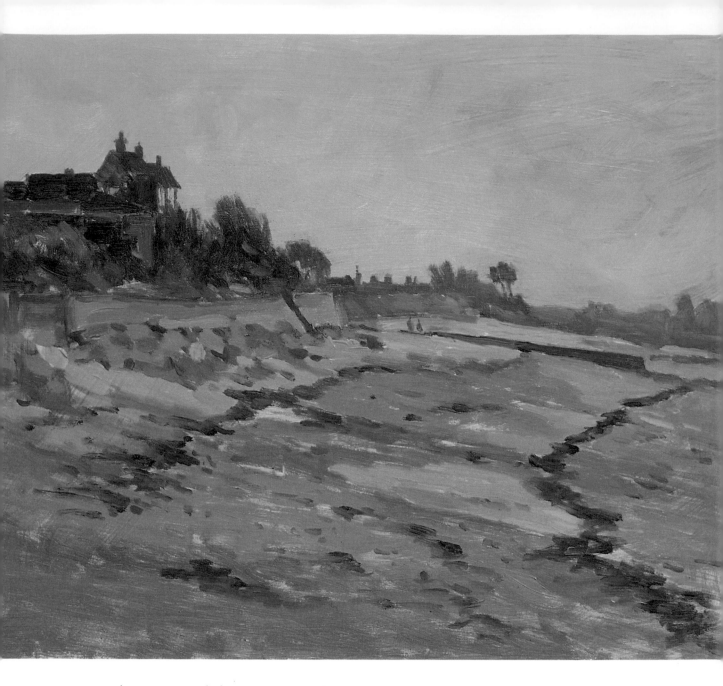

Early morning sunlight, Le Bourg, St Clement, Jersey. Oil on hardboard, 25 × 30 cm (10 × 12 in)